# 100 THINGS
# FLORIDA FANS
## SHOULD KNOW & DO
## BEFORE THEY DIE

# 100 THINGS FLORIDA FANS
# SHOULD KNOW & DO
# BEFORE THEY DIE

Pat Dooley

TRIUMPH
BOOKS

Library of Congress Cataloging-in-Publication Data

Dooley, Pat.
100 things Florida fans should know & do before they die / Pat Dooley.
   pages cm.
ISBN 978-1-60078-849-9
1. University of Florida—Football—History. 2. Florida Gators (Football team)—History. 3. University of Florida—Football—Anecdotes. 4. Florida Gators (Football team)—Anecdotes. I. Title. II. Title: One hundred things Florida fans should know and do before they die.
   GV958.U523.D645 2013
   796.332'6309759—dc23
                                                    2013011200

This book is available in quantity at special discounts for your group or organization. For further information, contact:

**Triumph Books LLC**
814 North Franklin Street
Chicago, Illinois 60610
(312) 337-0747
www.triumphbooks.com

Printed in U.S.A.
ISBN: 978-1-60078-849-9
Design by Patricia Frey
Photos courtesy of Getty Images unless otherwise indicated

*This book is dedicated to Marjorie Ann Dooley,*
*the best mother a guy could ask for.*

# Contents

# Foreword

I was torn. A critical decision was before me—a crossroads in my life—and I didn't know what to do.

It was February of 1992. I was a senior at Fort Walton Beach High School in the panhandle of Florida, and I had to choose whether to accept a scholarship from Florida or Florida State. Of course, from where I sit today, it's hard to even believe it was a tough decision at all. But as an 18-year-old without strong ties to either school, I really didn't know what to do. In the end both the opportunity to play quarterback for Steve Spurrier and attend such an incredibly impressive academic institution at UF tipped the scales for me.

I chose UF, and thank God I did!

When I look back on my football career, I often wonder if it really happened or if I was caught up in some amazing dream. We won rings, championships, and trophies, and we made lifetime friendships along the way. I also remain grateful for the great education I received at UF. Before I landed on my final major, public relations, I considered several other subjects. I could have chosen just about any major, and UF had one of the leading colleges in the country in that field. What a blessing! The University of Florida has had incredible athletic success over the years, but you'll never hear someone say we are only a "football school." UF is, without a doubt, a first-rate university that competes with just about any other school in the country.

But as the years have gone by—and they seem to pass by more and more quickly these days—another aspect to being a Gator has emerged for me. Being a Gator is more than an education or a college football career. Being a Gator is like being part of a large integrated family that is interwoven through all aspects of life and spans the entire country and beyond.

The support and encouragement I have received from Gator Nation has transcended my football career. When my wife and I lost everything we owned because of Hurricane Katrina, when Desire Street Ministries was under water, when my body shut down and became partially paralyzed with a rare autoimmune disorder called Guillain-Barre Syndrome—it was the Gator Nation that rallied with love and support.

In all kinds of weather, we all did stick together. It's more than a nice song after the third quarter of a football game. It's my experience as a Gators player.

So when I think back to my dilemma in 1992, it doesn't even seem like there should have been any choice at all. God led me to UF, and I am so grateful. I don't think God is a Gator or that you have to be a Gator to get into heaven…but why take that chance?

I know you'll love the opportunity to journey with my friend, Pat Dooley, as he relives some of the greatest moments in Gators history in this book. Pat brings back to life many of the moments that we all remember and he even introduces us to some new ones along the way. So sit back, enjoy the ride, and never forget how great it is to be a Florida Gator!

—Danny Wuerffel

# Introduction

I thought I had written my last book. But when the great people at Triumph Books approached me with the idea of writing this one, I accepted. I liked the concept and I have always been a sucker for lists (as you will see throughout this book).

The reason I thought I was finished writing books is because they are so labor-intensive, and my job covering Florida athletics has no real downtime. All of Florida's great athletic programs keep me busy. Not that I'm complaining. Covering Florida has been a boost for my career, my enjoyment, and my Marriott Rewards. And when it comes to writing about football—well, that's one reason I wanted to write this book.

I went to my first game in 1962. I sold hot dogs at the stadium. I took journalism classes in the stadium when the classrooms were still there. I was there for Steve Spurrier's kick and Emmitt Smith's runs and Tim Tebow's Promise.

I was there for all three national championship wins and consider myself fortunate to have covered Spurrier, the most unique person I have ever met. Whenever the sportswriters sit around a hospitality room at a Florida bowl game, the Spurrier stories start to flow. And as someone who has played a lot of golf with the head coach, I can tell you his competitiveness never stops.

We were playing in Washington, D.C., at a course called Raspberry Falls when Spurrier was coaching the Redskins. I was up a shot on him and hit a perfect drive down the middle of the 18th hole. "You gotta go for it in two now, Pat," he said. I got up to the ball and smacked my second shot at the green—except I didn't know there was water in front of it. *Splash.* And then he laid up short of the water and made a birdie and beat me by a shot.

It was on that trip that I saw the side of Spurrier that a lot of people don't see. He knew I had been diagnosed with prostate cancer, and this was my last assignment before surgery. Spurrier gave me the run of Redskins headquarters. At one point I was in a coach's office when I heard him coming down the hall. I heard Spurrier say, "Let's see if Pat Dooley's in here."

And in he walked, dragging Daniel Snyder, the Redskins owner. Spurrier treated me like a king over three days, and I've always been grateful to him for that. I've had great relationships with all of the Florida coaches, and it has been a real joy to cover the Gators over the years.

It isn't always easy. But it has been a blast.

Unfortunately, during the writing of this book, I lost my mother. She was the first person who saw in me the ability to write. She always knew I'd be a sportswriter, even though I had no clue coming out of high school. I miss her every day.

I also had a hip replaced. That made writing a little difficult, but I got it done.

I hope you enjoy this book. There are some stories in here that may surprise you; some of them surprised me. And in the end, I had one realization. Maybe all that Florida went through prior to 1990 made the last two-plus decades that much more enjoyable for the Gator Nation.

# 1 The 1996 National Championship

Florida football had long been referred to as the "sleeping giant" of college football, a term first coined by legendary Alabama coach Bear Bryant and sharpened by sportswriter Dan Jenkins. ("Florida has the arrogance of Alabama and the tradition of Wake Forest," he wrote.) Things changed a little in the 1980s and a lot in the 1990s. But there was one goal that eluded Florida until a series of events led the Gators to the sweetest path possible.

Florida's first national title was built as much on failure as success. Following a perfect 1995 regular season that included an SEC Championship win against Arkansas, the Gators were humiliated in the Fiesta Bowl by Nebraska 62–24 with a national championship on the line. For weeks they heard the joke, "Hey Gators, Nebraska just scored again."

It fueled them. "The entire offseason, the whole summer, everything we did was to keep that from happening again," said James Bates, a senior linebacker on the 1996 team. "We knew we had the talent to get back into that position again, and this time we were going to make sure we were prepared."

Florida lost some key players from the 1995 teams—most notably All-SEC wide receiver Chris Doering and left tackle Jason Odom. But quarterback Danny Wuerffel was back along with receivers Reidel Anthony and Ike Hilliard. The defense was solid, and Florida had added defensive coordinator Bobby Stoops to the staff.

For a good part of the season, it looked too easy. The Gators won in Knoxville, Tennessee, jumping out to a 35–0 lead before holding on for a 35–29 win. They went through an amazing stretch

1

against rivals LSU, Auburn, and Georgia, winning the three games by a combined 154–30.

Then it got hard.

Florida went to Tallahassee where the local paper's front page read "WAR!" in giant type. FSU was ranked second—one spot below the top-ranked Gators. The Seminoles were physical and relentless. They pounded Wuerffel and stifled Florida's offense. A late UF score made the final a respectable 24–21, but there was no doubt which team won the day. After the game Florida's sports information staff had to help Wuerffel into a chair for interviews. The dream was over. The team was beaten and its leader battered.

Those who covered the game knew that Wuerffel had taken a beating. Spurrier made sure the media knew just how bad. On the Tuesday following the game, he brought a handful of journalists into the coaches film room and showed them clips of the hits Wuerffel had taken from both the side view and the special end zone camera. Spurrier was incensed that so many of the hits came well after the ball had been thrown. When Chris Harry of the *Tampa Tribune* laughed at one of the more egregious late hits, Spurrier snapped, "Nothing funny about that, Chris. It's criminal."

Florida had to regroup just seven days later to play Alabama in the SEC Championship Game. It was that day that things started to happen. Texas, a 20-point underdog, stunned No. 3 Nebraska in the first ever Big 12 Championship Game. The Cornhuskers had played in three straight national title games, but the loss would eliminate them from the chance to play FSU in the Sugar Bowl and give Florida a chance to play in the game.

The Gators still had to win that night, and Wuerffel responded by throwing six touchdown passes against the Crimson Tide in an epic 45–30 victory.

Florida still needed some help because Arizona State, which would play Ohio State in the Rose Bowl, stood at No. 2 with an undefeated record. The night before the Sugar Bowl, Spurrier moved his team to little Gonzales, Louisiana, halfway between New Orleans and Baton Rouge, to get the players away from the hoopla of Bourbon Street. There the team watched Ohio State score a late touchdown to beat Arizona State. Players spilled into the hallways of the Gonzales Holiday Inn, screaming and hugging. It would be Florida vs. FSU for the national title. "We were excited," Wuerffel said. "But we also knew that none of it mattered if we didn't take care of business."

Gators fans stormed Bourbon Street after the Rose Bowl. The Florida band marched past the T-shirt shops and strip clubs while playing the fight song. The celebration began before the game had been played.

One night later Spurrier had a new twist for the Seminoles—the shotgun. The coach has been leery of the formation because he felt that a quarterback would be at a disadvantage if he had to take his eyes off the defense to see the ball coming to him. But he had tinkered with the shotgun in the weeks leading up to the Sugar Bowl.

He had something else, too. "I had my tackles back," Spurrier said. Both offensive tackles Zach Piller (before) and Mo Collins (during) had been injured when the two teams played during the regular season. With both players healthy and with the shotgun, Spurrier felt his offense could hum again.

And it did.

Wuerffel hit Hilliard with two first-half touchdown passes—the second on an amazing stop-and-go play where Hilliard caught a deep pass, put on the brakes, and let two FSU defenders fly by before cruising into the end zone. "I got hit right after I let it go, so I didn't realize what had happened until I looked at the big screen," Wuerffel said. "It was a phenomenal play by Ike."

Florida led only 24–20 after an FSU field goal early in the second half, but from then on it was all Florida. Wuerffel threw another touchdown pass to Hilliard, threading the needle from eight yards out. Terry Jackson punctuated the night with a 52-yard touchdown run that included a forward somersault into the end zone and later scored on a one-yard run.

As grown men wept in the stands, the Gators celebrated the 52–20 win on the field amidst the falling confetti. Wuerffel was mobbed by reporters when all he wanted to do was hug his teammates. "I was running all over the place," he said. "And the media guys were chasing me."

After the Gators retired to their Superdome locker room, Spurrier remembered something. It had been his custom to get a team picture after a championship was won, so he hustled the team back onto the artificial turf for the sweetest picture yet.

# 2 The Tebow Promise

The wait was longer than normal for the media assembled in the bowels of The Swamp. Urban Meyer had been in to explain what happened to his No. 1-ranked team. A handful of players had stopped by to answer a few questions in somber tones.

But where was the quarterback? Where was the unstoppable force who had been stopped on fourth-and-1 with the game on the line? Where was the young man who was not only the face of this Florida team but the face of college football?

The junior quarterback was in the locker room for a lot longer than normal. This was something he had not expected to experience. Sure, Florida had lost four games as a sophomore when he won the Heisman Trophy, but that Gators team wasn't ranked at the top. That team wasn't supposed to be one of the best ever at UF. "I sat at my locker for an hour, thinking about what I wanted

4

to say," Tim Tebow said later. "I learned a long time ago that in any situation, you have to find the positive. I wanted to let the Gator Nation know something good was going to come from this." As the media grew restless and wondered if Tebow was going to show, he strolled through the back door and in front of the cameras and tape recorders. Florida had just lost to Mississippi 31–30. Tebow had seemingly rallied the Gators late to avoid the unthinkable, but a blocked extra point left them short. The final rally ended at the Ole Miss 32-yard line with 41 seconds to play when Tebow was stuffed on a run to the right side.

Wearing a black T-shirt that matched the mood of the day, Tebow answered questions about the play, the loss, and the pain. "I want this to stay in our hearts and keep hurting," he said. "I don't want this to ever happen again." He looked down while he spoke, and his eyes glistened with the tears of disappointment. The last question came and went, and then he delivered what is now known as "the Promise."

"I just want to say one thing," he said. And then he paused to compose himself before delivering his speech with passion, poise, and a little bit of anger. "To the fans and everybody in Gator Nation, I'm sorry, extremely sorry. I promise you one thing—a lot of good will come out of this. You will never see any player in the entire country play as hard as I will play the rest of the season, and you will never see someone push the rest of the team as hard as I will push everybody the rest of the season, and you will never see a team play harder than we will the rest of the season. God bless."

At the time, it was a glorious clip for ESPN and juicy fodder for the few columnists in the room. Had Florida ended up in the Outback Bowl at the end of the season, it would hardly be remembered as a defining moment in Gators history.

But Florida won out. The Gators won what was a de facto national semifinal in the SEC Championship Game against Alabama when Tebow rallied Florida in the fourth quarter—something he had never done before. And Tebow and the Gators finished it off by beating Oklahoma in the BCS National Championship Game.

The Chosen One had delivered on the Promise.

Soon after the celebration to honor the 2008 championship, a stainless steel plaque was placed on the wall of the stadium near the entrance to the coaches offices and football museum. Tebow's speech was immortalized as a tribute to one of the greatest leaders the game has ever known as well as an inspiration to anyone who needs one.

Coaches at all levels—even rival SEC schools—have replayed the speech for their players when they need a boost. Before No. 1 Alabama's against Ole Miss in 2012, Tide coach Nick Saban had his team watch the Promise so they would not only understand the drive necessary to be successful but also the despair that comes with an upset loss.

# 3 The Heisman Fraternity

The way it has worked out, you might wonder why Florida would recruit any quarterbacks who are not the sons of preacher men. Three Florida quarterbacks have won the Heisman Trophy, college football's most coveted individual award. All of them had fathers who were ministers.

Steve Spurrier was the first to win the award in 1966. He had all of the necessary elements for a Heisman winner: gaudy statistics (for the time), a Heisman moment (a 40-yard field goal to beat

*Florida's three Heisman Trophy winners—Steve Spurrier, Tim Tebow, and Danny Wuerffel (from left to right)—pose with the coveted award.*

Auburn), and a great publicist (UF sports information director Norm Carlson). He also had the perfect initials—S.O.S. When the Gators were in trouble, the fans would send up a distress call for Stephen Orr Spurrier.

It would be 30 years before Florida would have another Heisman winner, and this time Spurrier would be coaching him. Danny Wuerffel was an Air Force brat whose father, Jon, often moved the family. The minister and his family finally settled in Fort Walton Beach, Florida, where Wuerffel became a high school phenom and a Florida State fan. But he was drawn to Spurrier's offense at Florida and as a senior put up numbers that were impossible for the voters to ignore.

Tim Tebow grew up a big Wuerffel fan and even had a poster of the Florida quarterback in his bedroom. It wasn't just the way Wuerffel played for the Gators, but the way he lived his life that was inspiring to Tebow. Tebow's father, Bob, has his ministry's home base in Jacksonville, Florida, but he also cared for children in the Philippines. Tebow was homeschooled but played for St. Augustine Nease High and was heavily recruited. He chose Florida over Alabama and spent 2006 as a situational quarterback for the national champions.

In 2007 Tebow did two things that had never been done before in college football. He became the first player to have more than 20 touchdown passes and 20 touchdown runs (32 passes and 23 runs) and became the first sophomore to ever win the Heisman.

The ceremonies for these three Heisman quarterbacks were quite different.

On the day he would find out he won the award, Spurrier had gone to class. In the afternoon, he was told to report to the office of university president J. Wayne Reitz. There he was told he had won the award. "I knew all along I had a pretty good chance," he said at the press conference.

Back then the voting was done before the regular season had finished. Florida still had a game to play against Miami. It turned

## Stiff-Armed—Gators Who Came Close

In addition to the three Florida quarterbacks who won the Heisman Trophy, five other Florida players have finished in the Top 10 in the voting. (Steve Spurrier, Danny Wuerffel, and Tim Tebow not only won the award, but they also had other years where they were in the top 10.)

- Fullback Jimmy DuBose finished sixth in 1975.
- Wide receiver Wes Chandler finished 10th in 1977.
- Running back Emmitt Smith finished ninth and seventh in 1987 and 1989, respectively.
- Quarterback Shane Matthews finished fifth in 1991.
- Quarterback Rex Grossman finished second in 2001.

Grossman and Tebow came the closest to adding a fourth trophy for the school. In 2001 Grossman was the favorite heading into the Tennessee game, which had been postponed until the end of the season because of the attacks of 9/11. Florida lost the game 34–32, and Grossman finished 62 points behind Nebraska quarterback Eric Crouch in the voting. Grossman, though, won the vote in both the Mid-Atlantic Region and the South Region.

In 2008—a year after winning the award—Tebow finished third despite receiving more first-place votes than winner Sam Bradford, the Oklahoma quarterback. Tebow had the last laugh as Florida beat Oklahoma in the national title game.

Tebow also finished fifth during his senior year in 2009. Spurrier finished ninth the year before he won it, and Wuerffel finished third the year before he won it.

out to be a 21–16 loss. One can't help but wonder if Purdue quarterback Bob Griese, the runner-up that year, might have benefitted from a later vote. Still, Spurrier flew to New York where he was formally presented with the stiff-armed trophy. Before the ceremony Jacksonville sportscaster Dick Stratton suggested to Spurrier that he give the trophy back to the university. Liking the idea, Spurrier did just that at the ceremony. Since that day the Downtown Athletic Club, which presents the award annually, adopted that strategy, giving out two trophies—one for the player and one for the school.

When Wuerffel won his Heisman, the announcement was carried live on television, and the result was in doubt. Despite Wuerffel's amazing numbers, many considered him a product of Spurrier's pass-friendly system. Wuerffel received 1,263 points, edging out Iowa State running back Troy Davis, who received 1,174. Wuerffel finished third in the West balloting behind Davis and Arizona State quarterback Jake Plummer.

On a cold night in New York City, Wuerffel and his family celebrated in a private dining room at the Downtown Athletic Club while the members of the club and the media covering the event bellied up to the bar a few feet away. One member of the media—Dave Sheinin of *The Miami Herald*—was trained in opera, and when Jon Wuerffel returned from the restroom on the way to the reserved dining room, the media members encouraged Sheinin to sing "Danny Boy" for the proud father. Sheinin later serenaded Danny to Jon's delight. "I knew eventually I'd find the talent in one of you guys," Danny quipped.

The 1996 presentation was one of the last at the Downtown Athletic Club, which was crippled by the attacks of 9/11. By the time Tebow won the award in 2007, the ESPN announcement took place at the Nokia Theater in Times Square. When Tebow was declared the winner, he hugged his parents and his coach. When he got to the stage, he was greeted by Wuerffel, who was there with other former Heisman winners, and the two exchanged big hugs. "I think it's amazing that you're known forever as a Heisman Trophy winner," Tebow said. "That's very special. It's overwhelming. I'm kind of at a loss for words."

# 4 Giddy in Glendale

For weeks they heard it. For weeks they chewed on it. And when the time came, they acted on it. The 2006 Gators didn't have to wait long for the questions to come about their worthiness in the BCS National Championship Game. Minutes after the announcement was made, ESPN's Kirk Herbstreit ripped the decision on the air, saying it should have been an Ohio State-Michigan rematch in Glendale, Arizona. And he wasn't alone. As a result Florida coach Urban Meyer made sure that every negative comment made about his Gators was tacked up on a bulletin board in their dining area. "You start messing around with people's pride, and I try not to watch, but for 30 days we have been watching it, too," Meyer said. "You start rubbing that for a day or two and you get over it. You do it for 30 days and you have a bunch of tigers. I really enjoyed coaching this team, and it wasn't hard [to motivate them] over the past 30 days."

The sparkling new University of Phoenix Stadium, which had opened the previous August, looked like a spaceship dropped into the desert. Inside the stadium the Gators played out of this world.

After Ohio State's Ted Ginn Jr. ran the opening kickoff back 93 yards for a score, nothing went right for the Buckeyes. Ginn suffered an ankle injury during the celebration of his touchdown and didn't play again. Ohio State was penalized on the ensuing kickoff for a face-mask tackle. Florida tied the game in a matter of minutes and never looked back. "I thought it was going to be a shootout after that kickoff return," senior quarterback Chris Leak said. "I knew that first drive was important."

Leak ended up the Most Valuable Player in the game, throwing for 213 yards and a score. Freshman Tim Tebow ran for one touchdown and threw for another. The Gators limited Ohio State to 82 total yards, and UF fans rubbed it in by buying coffee mugs and T-shirts with "82 yards" inscribed on them.

Florida sacked Heisman Trophy winner Troy Smith five times and stuffed a fourth-and-1 run by Beanie Wells that gave the Gators the ball in Ohio State territory. The play was an example of the speed advantage the Gators had over the Buckeyes. They left defensive end Ray McDonald unblocked, figuring he couldn't get to the ball carrier. McDonald sped into the backfield and grabbed Wells by the waist, negating any momentum he could generate. "We were faster than Ohio State," wide receiver Andre Caldwell said. "They didn't want to face the reality of it. But that was the reality."

Florida's 41–14 win erased any questions about whether the Gators belonged in the title game. Tebow's 1-yard touchdown pass to Caldwell just before the end of the first half virtually clinched the game, and his 1-yard touchdown run was the only score of the second half. After a season full of tension and tight games, this team finally enjoyed a breather. "This was the easiest game we played all year," McDonald said.

As the confetti dropped and the crystal was presented, Meyer hugged his senior quarterback by the neck. "We'll be joined at the hip forever," Meyer said.

Previous coach Ron Zook had brought the highly recruited quarterback to UF, and Leak's transformation from a quiet follower to a vocal leader had been a struggle for Meyer. But it ended with the ultimate win. "It was really overwhelming," Leak said. "It was like a big weight off my shoulders."

For Meyer it was the first of two national championships. But it wasn't until late in the game that he realized what he had accomplished in his second year as the Florida coach. "Everyone was celebrating behind me, and I was screaming on the headsets

## Titletown

The Florida Gators sure know how to celebrate an anniversary.

In 2006 UF celebrated 100 years of its football program with all kinds of ceremonies, including the unveiling of the Ring of Honor and bringing back the 1996 national championship team. But the Year of the Gator was much more than pomp and circumstance.

In April Florida's basketball team won its first national title by beating UCLA. Four days later the four sophomores, who were the stars of the team, asked the crowd if they should come back for another year. Finally, center Joakim Noah yelled into the microphone, "Let it be done then. We back, baby!" When Florida defeated Ohio State in the BCS national championship game, UF became the first school ever to hold both the football and basketball titles at the same time.

Also in 2006:

- Former UF player David Eckstein was named the MVP of the World Series for the victorious St. Louis Cardinals.
- Former UF players Udonis Haslem and Jason Williams helped the Miami Heat win an NBA title.
- And former UF running back Emmitt Smith won *Dancing With the Stars*.

It was such a glorious year that the nickname "Titletown" stuck with the city of Gainesville.

because the game wasn't over," Meyer said. "There's one play I'll never forget. We had a third-and-6 late in the game. We threw a bubble screen to Percy Harvin. I remember they stretched out the chains, and we had the first down, and it just hit me. My legs started shaking uncontrollably. *We just won a national championship.* I'll never forget that."

If there was one signature play in the game, it came on a play that would have resulted in a penalty today. Linebacker Earl Everett was rushing the passer, and an Ohio State offensive lineman knocked off his helmet. That didn't slow Everett, who chased down

Smith from behind to sack him. (A rule change in 2012 penalizes a player who keeps playing after losing his helmet.) On the Fox broadcast of the game, commentator Charles Davis said, "'I don't need no stinkin' helmet,' says Earl Everett."

# The First "Official" SEC Title

Florida had won the SEC three times prior to the 1991 season. There was only one problem: None of them counted.

In 1984 the Gators were stripped of their title in a vote of the other nine conference schools because of numerous NCAA violations. That also made the Gators ineligible the following year when they went 5–1 in the SEC. And in Steve Spurrier's first year, previous violations resulted in Florida accepting a penalty that prohibited bowl and conference crown eligibility. Florida, however, finished with the league's best record again, setting it up for a run in '91. "We were in the meeting early in the season with [UF president] John Lombardi, and he asked me if I thought we had a chance to win the SEC," Spurrier said. "And I told him that we'd already beaten Alabama, and if we could split with Auburn and Georgia, we probably could. And there was a dean there, and he stood up and said, 'We've never won the SEC. Why would you think we could do it this year?'

"Every time I see him I tell him, 'Oh ye of little faith.'"

Florida also handled Alabama at home in 1991 in a game that had plenty of pregame controversy. *The Birmingham News* columnist Charles Hollis had written that Spurrier bragged to a Gator Club that they would beat the Tide by 30 points. Spurrier sent a letter to Alabama coach Gene Stallings, assuring him that he never said any such thing. It turned out Spurrier underestimated his team. Florida won 35–0.

The Gators followed that up with a 16–0 shutout win against LSU. In one of the loudest games played at Ben Hill Griffin Stadium, Florida beat Tennessee 35–18. Defensive back Larry Kennedy clinched the win with an interception return for a touchdown.

The biggest barrier for Florida teams in the past had been the difficult quiniela of Auburn and Georgia back-to-back. The Auburn game was always intense and physical, and so many UF teams had been unable to sustain the energy for two straight weeks. This team was different. The Gators pounded Auburn 31–10 and embarrassed Georgia 45–13.

All they had to do now was beat Kentucky at home to win their first official SEC title. When Florida went up big early, the celebration began. But Kentucky, with a dual-threat quarterback in Pookie Jones, rallied to make things interesting. The Wildcats, who came into the game with an 0–6 SEC record, cut the lead to 32–26.

Florida badly needed a first down to change the momentum. On a third-down play, the call was for quarterback Shane Matthews to hit running back Errict Rhett in the middle of the field. Matthews was pressured and threw the ball before Rhett turned around, but fortunately for the Gators, Rhett turned around in the nick of time to make the catch and get the first down. Florida drove to a field goal, and Kentucky's comeback ran out of time. On the game's final play, Jones threw a one-hopper short of his receiver in the end zone, and the Gators could finally celebrate. They slapped on "SEC Champions" hats and reveled in the moment. Spurrier grabbed a microphone to thank the fans. "Thanks for hanging around," he said. "We needed you there at the end. The Lord has smiled on us all season, and that last drive he smiled on us again."

In only his second season as the Florida coach, Spurrier had done what he was unable to do as a player and what no coach before him at UF had been able to do…officially. As fans chanted "S-E-C," nose tackle Brad Culpepper reminded the fans that they still had another game to play. And a week later, Florida beat No. 3-ranked Florida State to finish the regular season with a 10–1 record.

A Sugar Bowl loss to Notre Dame was hardly the way this team wanted to go out, but it will always be remembered as the first Gators team to win a conference title.

# 6 Florida's Third National Championship

The game was long over. Players were finished making confetti snow angels on the floor of Sun Life Stadium in Miami Gardens, Florida. The crystal had been presented. The fans were navigating the congestion on their drive home. And Tim Tebow was ready to answer questions about the game and what had happened to his voice.

Tebow was hoarse, his words coming out raspily as he dodged the question about his damaged throat. It wouldn't be until many days later when a video was released that we found out why.

With the score tied at 7 and the second half about to begin, Tebow huddled his offense and started screaming like he was a WWE wrestler. "Get in here! Get in here right now! Thirty minutes for the rest of your life! That's our bad in the first half. That ain't happening, I promise you. We get the ball. I promise you one thing: We're going to hit somebody and we're going to move the ball down the field and score a touchdown. I guarantee you that. Look at me! Look at me! We got 30 minutes for the rest of our lives. Thirty minutes for the rest of our lives! Let's go!"

The junior quarterback's face had turned crimson by the time he finished exhorting his teammates. Whether his speech was the inspiration or not, Florida made all of the big plays in the second half and won the game 24–14. Oklahoma had set a national record for points scored in a season with 702 but could only manage a pair of touchdown passes from Heisman Trophy winner Sam Bradford to tight end Jermaine Gresham. The Sooners had 25 first downs, but they suffered a blocked field goal, failed to convert a fourth-and-goal at the 2-yard line, and threw two interceptions, including one near the goal line late in the first half.

Meanwhile Florida's Percy Harvin gave Florida an offensive boost. After missing the SEC Championship Game with a fracture in his ankle, he spent the Christmas holidays in the training room, working to get back and he rushed for 122 yards and a score, even though he was less than 100 percent. Tebow threw a pair of touchdown passes in the game—the last one was a jump pass to David Nelson that clinched it.

Florida's defensive coordinator Charlie Strong had used a unique way to fire up his troops, walking through the players as they ate their pregame meal and telling Tebow in a loud voice that he had better be ready to score a lot of points because the defense couldn't handle Oklahoma's offense.

The season, though, would become known for another speech, one of several moments on the way to the title game. Tebow delivered "the Promise" after the loss to Ole Miss, but it wasn't like it immediately inspired the team. The following week in Fayetteville, Arkansas, Florida struggled with an unranked Arkansas team. When Tebow threw a clutch touchdown pass to Harvin early in the fourth quarter, the quarterback walked off the field with no excitement. He was angry about some earlier mistakes. Florida coach Urban Meyer threw his arms in the air to try to fire up Tebow, and the quarterback responded with a chest bump. "It hurt a little," Meyer said.

From that point on, Florida was a juggernaut. On the third play of the next game against fourth-ranked LSU, Tebow hit

Harvin with a 70-yard touchdown pass, and Florida went on to win 51–21. The Gators beat Kentucky the next week 63–5.

Then came Georgia.

The previous year the Bulldogs had scored first in the game, and Georgia coach Mark Richt sent the entire team onto the field to celebrate in an attempt to fire up Dawg Nation. Georgia won the game 42–30, and Meyer was not thrilled with the gesture. During the week of the Florida-Georgia game in 2008, Meyer had a dream that Florida was handling Georgia and he instructed Tebow to take a snap and throw the ball as hard as he could into the Georgia section. Instead as the waning minutes were ticking off of a 49–10 Florida win, Meyer twice called timeout to make the Bulldogs stay on the field and endure the humiliating loss.

The Florida onslaught continued as the Gators handled Vanderbilt 42–14 and then dispatched of nemesis—and former coach—Steve Spurrier and his Gamecocks 56–6. After scoring 70 against The Citadel, Florida had climbed from a ranking of No. 12, following the Ole Miss loss, to second in the nation.

On a rainy day in Tallahassee, the Gators rolled 45–15. But that game will be remembered for Tebow's *Braveheart* moment. After Harvin went down with an injury and writhed in pain on the ground, Florida State fans cheered. So Tebow took matters into his own hands, moving the pile on a quarterback rush until the ball was in the end zone. When he came up from the mass of humanity, Tebow was covered in the paint used to decorate the end zone. It looked like blood was pouring from his ear as if he had just fought a battle for Scotland, but it was actually just garnet paint. Tebow went down the sideline, throwing his arms up in the air to fire up the crowd.

Florida came from behind to beat No. 1 Alabama in Atlanta the following week 31–20.

# 7 Danny Wonderful

It's almost impossible to talk about one without the other. Danny Wuerffel did things on a football field that hadn't been done by any Gator before him, and yet it's the off-the-field stuff that explains who he is as a person.

A deeply religious man, Wuerffel offered his symbol of faith after throwing touchdown passes—his hands clasped together in prayer followed by a look to the sky. He had plenty of chances to do that, throwing for an SEC-record 114 touchdowns during his four seasons at Florida. He was the winner of the Draddy Award that goes to college football's top scholar-athlete and, of course, the Heisman Trophy. But he would make a bigger mark on humankind after his career at Florida.

The New Orleans Saints drafted Wuerffel, and the first thought on the minds of every Gators fan was, "Really?" The Big Easy is about as opposite from Wuerffel's lifestyle as you can get. When he came to Florida on his recruiting visit, Wuerffel insisted on being taken to the movies rather than the clubs. But as he would find out, there was a reason for his New Orleans relocation. It wasn't just that he had won the national championship on the same field where the Saints play. It wasn't just that the Saints had a mess of a quarterback situation that would push him into the starting lineup early in the season.

New Orleans needed him.

Out of college and eager to make a mark, Wuerffel wanted to go somewhere and see real poverty. He was taken to the Ninth Ward in New Orleans not far from the Louisiana Superdome. "It was pretty bad," he said. "And then a young girl came out of

## Doering's Got a Touchdown!

Danny Wuerffel threw 1,170 passes during his four years at Florida, and many were memorable. But one of them was unforgettable.

Seventh-ranked Florida trailed unranked Kentucky 20–17 in 1993 thanks in part to seven interceptions thrown by Wuerffel and starter Terry Dean in the game. The Gators had one last chance with just more than a minute to go, and Wuerffel was given the nod to go under center. He completed three passes to move the ball to the Kentucky 28-yard line, but with eight seconds to go, it didn't look good for the Gators.

On the previous play, walk-on wide receiver Chris Doering had run straight down the field but was held up by the Kentucky linebacker. Steve Spurrier called the same play, and this time Doering was allowed to run unimpeded. Wuerffel hit Doering with a perfect pass near the goal line with three seconds remaining, and Florida had escaped. The call from UF play-by-play man Mick Hubert bounced off the walls of the radio booth at Commonwealth Stadium: *Doering's got a touchdown! Doering's got a touchdown!*

Who knows what might have happened had Wuerffel not hit on that pass? Florida went on to win its second SEC title and play in the Sugar Bowl. Although Dean regained the quarterback duties later in the season, eventually Wuerffel would be the starter in 1994 and throughout the next two seasons.

this condemned building carrying a doll, and I realized she lived there."

The experience revealed to Wuerffel what he should do, and he started Desire Street Ministries. Its mission "is to encourage and equip leaders to transform impoverished neighborhoods through spiritual and community development." Wuerffel worked hard to get a community center built. This wasn't a public relations move. He spent plenty of time there, playing catch with the kids who frequented the center. "One time I threw a kid a pass, and he asked me if I ever played quarterback," Wuerffel said. "I just said, 'Yeah, a little bit.'"

The Ninth Ward was one of the hardest areas hit when Hurricane Katrina hit New Orleans. Wuerffel had moved his family into the area to be closer to those in need, and his house was destroyed. So was the community center. But Wuerffel remained upbeat. He told anyone who would listen that his family was safe, and that was all that mattered. He relocated to Atlanta and continued to spread the word of Desire Street. There are now branches in Dallas; Montgomery, Alabama; Lakeland, Florida; and New Orleans. Wuerffel returned to Gainesville on several occasions and sometimes would bring one of the success stories from Desire Streets for a Gator game.

All was well until the summer of 2011 when Wuerffel was diagnosed with Guillain-Barre Syndrome, a disease that attacks the immune system. The once-strapping quarterback had to spend a lot of time in bed and was forced to put his work on hold while he tried to get healthy. He fought back and made it to his Desire Street Golf Tournament at TPC Sawgrass in Ponte Vedra, Florida, though he was still too weak to play more than a few holes. "I see this as a gift," he said during his recovery. "I look at my life and see all that I was trying to do. The Lord forced me to slow down and reflect on some things. I want to be a good father and a good husband and impact lives for many years to come. At the pace I was going, I wouldn't have lasted in a healthy way. It has been humbling to go from a strong, healthy guy to someone who can't ride a bike or go swimming or go play soccer."

Wuerffel has recovered from the disease and continues to make an impact on the lives of the impoverished.

# Coach Spurrier Shakes Up the SEC

Everyone knew things were going to be different at that first press conference. Florida was welcoming back its favorite son to be the new head coach of the Gators, and he already was changing things. Florida would go back to blue jerseys. The orange ones "look too much like Clemson," Spurrier said. The artificial turf was too dangerous; Florida would play its games on grass. And Spurrier wanted to renew the series with Miami. But nobody had any idea how different it was about to get at UF...and in the SEC.

The league had long been known for physical defense and grind-it-out offense. Spurrier believed in "pitching it around." The Gator fans got a dose of what they were in for on the first offensive play he called—Trips Left Zip Blue Slide Red Cross, a deep pass from Shane Matthews to Ernie Mills. Three plays later Florida was in the end zone.

The Gators walloped Oklahoma State in Spurrier's UF debut 50–7. After the game the media got a taste of what was to come when Spurrier said, "We knew Oklahoma State wasn't very good."

His candor continued throughout his Florida career, often angering the opposition. But he was able to back up his jabs with success. Florida, which had never won the SEC title, won in 1991, '93, '94, '95, '96, and 2000. The Gators twice played for the national title, winning it in 1996. Florida led the SEC in scoring seven times in Spurrier's 12 years. Spurrier acknowledged that he inherited a lot of good players from former coach Galen Hall's recruiting "especially on defense." But the style was all his own.

He was a big believer in Sun Tzu's *The Art of War*, especially the quotes, "All war is deception," and "If your opponent is of choleric temper, seek to irritate him." So when Florida State had an issue with players receiving free merchandise from an athletic store, he referred to them as "Free Shoes U." And when Tennessee kept losing to the Gators and falling into the Citrus Bowl, he said, "You can't spell Citrus without UT." After a win over Ray Goff's Georgia team in 1991, he really got under the coach's skin with this quote—"Why is it that during recruiting season they sign all the great players, but when it comes time to play the game, we have all the great players? I don't understand that. What happens to them?"

After the Vols had lost to Memphis and Florida was cruising to another SEC East title in 1996, he handed a cartoon, which he had received, to a writer. It listed Tennessee's goals for the season, and each had been crossed out until the last line.

~~National Champions~~
~~SEC Champions~~
~~SEC East Champions~~
~~State Champions~~
Knox Co. Champions

Spurrier finished with a 122–27–1 record before leaving for the NFL. He certainly was not the most patient coach on the sidelines. He once punted on third down because he was "tired of watching our offense." After quarterback Jesse Palmer missed an open player on a long pass, Spurrier turned to backup Rex Grossman and asked, "Can you hit that guy?" When Grossman replied that he could, Spurrier sent him into the game.

The quarterbacks who were the most successful for Spurrier were the ones who could filter the noise. "You take it all in," Danny Wuerffel said, "but only pay attention to the parts that were going to make you better."

Spurrier wasn't afraid to go after coaches he felt were doing things the wrong way. He stood up at the SEC coaches meeting in Destin, Florida, and accused Alabama coach Mike DuBose of cheating. He battled with *Orlando Sentinel* columnist Larry Guest until he refused to answer any of Guest's questions. When Guest questioned Spurrier at the press conference before the 1994 SEC Championship Game, Spurrier said, "Why do you even try?"

Try as you might, you will never find another coach like Spurrier in the SEC or—for that matter—college football.

# The Gator Chomp

When President Barack Obama was campaigning for a second term in 2012, he stopped at a Gators Dockside restaurant in Orlando. And during his informal talk with potential voters, he performed the Gator Chomp—a savvy political move.

The Chomp has become one of the most popular and recognizable gestures in sports, so simple and yet so perfect—arms stretched out in front of you, top palm turned down, and bottom palm turned up. Now…Chomp.

Although the history of the football program goes back more than 100 years, the Chomp is relatively new in comparison. It was used by cheerleaders for their cheer, "Eat 'Em Up, Gators, Eat 'Em Up" in the 1970s but never really caught on with the fans. Then in 1981 Florida played Mississippi State in Jackson, Mississippi. The Mississippi State band was playing the theme from *Jaws*, the popular 1975 movie, and the Florida pep band made special notice of it. Monty Musgrave, a member of the pep band, and Rob Hyatt, the director of the pep band, looked at each other and knew it had to be incorporated at UF.

*Cheerleaders perform the Gator Chomp, a gesture which has become synonymous with University of Florida sports.*

At the next band meeting, Musgrave asked to write the music for the tuba section. The pep band introduced it at the next game—on the road at Louisiana State—and let the cheerleaders know that was a good time to do their version of the chomp. The Gators fans, who attended the next home game against Maryland, were quick to catch on, and a tradition was born.

Versions of the Gator Chomp have sprung up around the nation at different schools. Florida had to deal with a letter of copyright infringement from the composer of the theme, John Williams. So the band changed the name of their song from "Gator Jaws" to "Gator Chomp." The Chomp has become the symbol of the Gator Nation. Comedians and musicians who perform in Gainesville are almost required to do a chomp or two. It hasn't been unusual to see professional golfers such as former UF student-athletes Chris DiMarco and Camilo Villegas doing the Chomp as they walk down the fairway after a good shot.

High school seniors use it as a way of announcing that they are committing to Florida. Opponents use it as a way to taunt the Gators. Usually in those cases, the Chomp is followed by a throat slash (See: Miami's Brock Berlin in the 2003 game against Florida.) And in gymnastics UF All-American Colleen Johnson decided in 1994 to incorporate a Chomp into her floor routine. It is now part of every Florida gymnasts' floor routine and is met with a loud collective Chomp from the Gator crowd.

# 10 Urban Legend

It was one of those summer Gator Club meetings where everybody gets fired up about the upcoming season. It was August of 2012 in Treasure Beach, Florida, and before the main speaker went up, there was a raffle. One of the prizes? An autographed picture of Urban Meyer. When the emcee held it up, everybody booed. The wound was still too fresh for this group of Gators. Who knows when and if it will ever scab over?

The legacy of Meyer is one of the most complicated ones in college football history. How can a coach who won two national titles, beat the snot out of Florida's biggest rivals, and recruited its most beloved player be so reviled?

It's not an across-the-board anger directed at Meyer. There are many in the Gator Nation who appreciate what he did as a Gator coach. The man went 65–15, including 17–2 against UF's rivals. He won five out of six bowl games—two of them on college football's biggest stage. He also went 36–5 at home.

But it's the way he left. Maybe time will change things. "I want to be accepted back there one day," he said. One day he will go into the Ring of Honor, a place reserved for only the best of the best. What will that reception be like?

Some of it is Meyer's fault. For as much as he preached family, he never warmed up to the fan base. Meyer was so focused on his football team that he became a closed person around anyone else. That included the media, many of whom are still taking shots at him. He had a few close friends. One of them was Drew Copeland of the band Sister Hazel. Copeland would take his guitar to Meyer's lake house, which was on Melrose Bay and 15 minutes from the Florida football offices, and play music on the dock.

In the summer of 2009, with two national titles tucked away, Meyer talked about how much he loved Gainesville and that he knew it was his dream job. "This is it," he said.

A few months later, he resigned.

After guiding the Gators to a 12–0 mark, he watched Alabama handle his team in the SEC Championship Game. Back home in Gainesville that night, he woke up and sat upright in bed, then fell to the floor. His wife called 911, and Meyer was taken to the hospital.

He resigned the day before the Gators left for the Sugar Bowl. Less than 24 hours later, he changed his mind. Meyer said he was

## Meyer's Traditions

Urban Meyer had about as much to do with changing the way Florida's football program went about its business as any coach in Florida history. Meyer was at UF for six years and introduced so many features that are now part of Florida football.

- **The Gator Walk.** Other schools conduct a similar activity, but Florida didn't do it before Meyer. The team buses pull up on University Avenue north of the stadium, and the players walk through a gauntlet of fans. The most memorable was before the 2008 LSU game when quarterback Tim Tebow bounced through the crowd screaming in an effort to fire them up.
- **The Singing.** There didn't used to be many people in Gator Nation who even knew the words of the fight song, but they do now. Meyer started the practice of having his team sing the alma mater and the Gators fight song with the Florida band after victories.
- **The Champions Dinner.** Play like a champion, you get steak and nice silverware. If you don't, you're eating hot dogs with plastic forks.
- **The BBQ.** Meyer wanted to embrace the past at Florida and invited all former players to come back to the school for a barbecue lunch prior to the season.

impressed with how hard his team practiced that morning despite the news that their coach was leaving. He claimed he was going to try to delegate more, spend more time with his family, and see if it worked. Meyer looked spaced out and gaunt during Sugar Bowl week, and after Florida thrashed Cincinnati he looked out of it on the winner's platform.

But after taking an overseas trip and spending a lot of time at the lake house, Meyer declared himself fit and ready to go for the 2010 season. The trouble was that he had lost so much. Florida had nine players drafted that April, and Charlie Strong had left to become the head coach at Louisville. On the field Florida tried to run the offense it had with Tebow, but quarterback John Brantley was a drop-back passer with limited mobility. Florida went 8–5. Meyer had not experienced a season like this. He talked about "rebuilding this the right way," but a few days after the season, he resigned again.

Meyer said he wanted to spend more time with his family but told *The Gainesville Sun* that his health concerns were a big part of his reason to step down. He took a job working for ESPN, played a lot of golf, coached his son's Little League team, and watched his daughters play college volleyball.

But then Jim Tressel was fired at Ohio State, and the rumors started. Meanwhile, Will Muschamp's first Florida team, the one he inherited from Meyer, was a mess. The easy answer was that Meyer had left the cupboard bare. "All I did for six years is go into that office every day and work my tail off," Meyer said. "And then I go out to get a sandwich, and somebody is yelling at me because they had a bunch of false start penalties."

When Meyer took the Ohio State job, it got ugly in the Gator Nation. The perception, whether true or false, was that Meyer had walked away from a sinking ship. In a way, it was the best thing that could have happened to Muschamp. Gators fans had someone else to blame for a 7–6 season. There were Florida fans who found themselves rooting for whoever Ohio State played. There had been an underlying rivalry between the two schools because of the national title games in football and basketball, but this development made it explode.

Florida returned to the Sugar Bowl in 2012 under Muschamp. They won 11 games, so clearly Meyer left talent behind. And in a way, Florida winning again was the best thing that could have happened for Meyer.

# 11 The Title That Didn't Count

It was hardly the perfect start to what would become one of the greatest seasons in Florida history. In the summer of 1984, the NCAA was getting closer to nailing Florida coach Charley Pell for recruiting violations. Then his top three quarterbacks suffered major injuries, leaving him with a walk-on starter at the position. Then the Gators lost a heartbreaker in Tampa, Florida, to Miami.

Charley Pell's final season as the UF coach lasted only three games. With a record of 1–1–1, Pell resigned after the NCAA charged Florida with 106 violations following its 30-month investigation. Pell swore until his death in 2001 that the biggest mistake he made was "taking the blame and cutting a deal to save my staff."

Part of that staff was a newly hired offensive coordinator named Galen Hall, who was not cited in any of the violations, and Florida named him interim head coach. In a lot of ways, it was the perfect storm. Florida was loaded with talent, and Hall's laid-back approach fit well with players accustomed to Pell's serious and sometimes uptight demeanor. With Hall at the controls, the Gators rolled. The walk-on quarterback, Kerwin Bell, began to shine, and Florida's defense was vicious.

The Gators finished the season ranked ninth in the nation in offense and 14th in defense. Under Hall, Florida won all eight games it played in 1984 to finish 9–1–1. One of the biggest games was a nationally televised 24–3 win against Auburn. The offense, led by tailback Neal Anderson, had its way with the 11th-ranked Tigers, and the defense stuffed Auburn. Anderson had fumbled three times in a 28–21 loss to the Tigers the year before but scored a pair of touchdowns in the win. After the game Florida fans chanted," S-E-C! S-E-C!" and Gators players waved to the skybox where Pell was watching.

There, though, was still work to do. Georgia, unbeaten in conference play, didn't have Herschel Walker anymore, but the Bulldogs were still ranked eighth in the country and had beaten Florida six straight times. The Gators rolled to a 27–0 win fueled by a goal-line stand, and that victory featured a 96-yard touchdown pass from Bell to Ricky "the Rocket" Nattiel. Gators fans stormed the field after the game and tore down the goalposts.

All Florida had to do was beat Kentucky in Lexington, Kentucky, to clinch their first ever SEC title. The Wildcats battled to the end when Florida safety Adrian White picked off a pass to preserve the 25–17 win. After all these years, Florida had finally won an SEC title. As the players celebrated in the locker room, UF president Marshall Criser announced that the interim tag was coming off Hall's title. He would serve as the Gators coach. The players did not truly understand the significance of their title until arriving back home. The pilot of their chartered aircraft flew low over Ben Hill Griffin Stadium, so the players could see a lighted stadium half-filled with fans waiting for their arrival. "That was the most incredible thing I've ever seen," Bell said.

Florida beat Florida State to close the season at 9–1–1. The players received their championship rings, Florida was awarded the trophy, and after the bowl games, *The New York Times* presented Florida with a national championship trophy based on its own poll. But that spring at the SEC meeting in Destin, Florida, the Tennessee contingent pushed to have the title vacated because Florida had been on probation during the season. By a vote of 6–4, the league's presidents voted that way. Tennessee also pushed to have Florida's record eradicated from the official SEC standings, but the league didn't go that far, instead listing Florida at the top of the standings with a symbol and an explanation: ^ *Championship vacated*. "We all know who won the SEC that year," Bell said. "I still have my ring. We won it on the field."

Because of the two years of probation, Florida was also ineligible to compete for the SEC title in 1985 as well. Florida's 5–1 conference record was the same as Tennessee's, and the Gators beat the Vols during that season. But the conference championship went to Tennessee. No wonder the Vols pushed for Florida's ineligibility.

# 12 Meyer-Spurrier II

The 2006 season did not start with the lofty expectations of a national title. Florida was ranked in the top 10 of both the coaches (eighth) and writers (seventh) polls in Urban Meyer's second year, but other teams were getting the preseason love. Ohio State was loaded. So was Southern Cal. Florida? The Gators had lost three road games the previous year, and this season seemed to be more of the same. "I was very concerned offensively," Meyer said. "I knew with [co-coordinators] Greg Mattison and Charlie Strong in their second year we'd be really good on defense. But I wasn't sure about the offense."

Freshmen Tim Tebow and Percy Harvin gave Florida the lift it needed on offense. Senior quarterback Chris Leak was able to put his ego aside and allow Tebow to run short-yardage plays, and Harvin had the ability to explode whether he was playing wide receiver or running back. Still this was a team based on defense. And when that defensive effort was not good enough on a rough night in Auburn, Alabama, things began to unravel.

A controversial play was ruled a fumble. A bobbled snap on a punt gave Auburn a touchdown. A public address system blared rock music when the Gators were on offense (which was against SEC rules and led to an unprecedented warning from the league office). It added up to a 27–17 loss that included an Auburn defensive touchdown on the game's final play.

When Meyer finished his media obligations, he walked into a locker room unlike any he had ever seen. "People want to say that losing builds character," Meyer said. "Sometimes it exposes some deep-rooted feelings. There were some things that I didn't know were going on. There was an offense vs. defense thing. There were some cliques. I walked in, and it was almost fighting. Everybody was waiting for me to stop it. I wanted to let it go. It went on for 20 minutes. And then the air was cleared."

Florida dropped to ninth in the Associated Press poll after the loss. But teams started losing, and Florida started winning again and clinched the SEC East with a win at Vanderbilt. Next up— South Carolina and Steve Spurrier.

In his first encounter against Florida, Spurrier had knocked his alma mater out of a chance to play in Atlanta in 2005 by beating the Gators in Columbia, South Carolina. And it looked like he would do it again this year. Florida struggled offensively, and the Gamecocks went up 16–10 in the fourth quarter. But defensive end Jarvis Moss blocked the extra point.

The Gators went on an 80-yard drive that took 11 plays with their season on the line. Tim Tebow scored on a 12-yard run, and Chris Hetland kicked the extra point to give UF the one-point lead. South Carolina marched right back down the field, and when quarterback Blake Mitchell hit a 12-yard pass to Freddie Brown to the UF 32-yard line, the Gators appeared doomed. After a running play lost three yards, Gamecocks offensive lineman Jamon Meredith was flagged for a false start, moving the ball back to the 40. Mitchell completed one more pass to put the ball on the Florida 31. Ryan Succop, who had already had a field goal and an extra point blocked, came in to win the game.

His 48-yard field goal attempt never crossed the goal line. Florida defensive tackles Ray McDonald and Steve Harris fired into the South Carolina line, allowing Moss some room to maneuver, and the 6'6" end jumped as high as he could, deflecting the ball with his meaty hand. It wobbled harmlessly to the 9-yard line where safety Tony Joiner jumped on it. Meyer had thought about calling a timeout to freeze Succop but said, "I couldn't stand it. I wanted to find out what was going to happen."

An exhausted Moss originally was supposed to come out on the play. But he begged Florida defensive coordinator Charlie Strong, who was also in charge of the field goal block unit, to stay in. "I wasn't coming out," he said. "Steve and Ray did the work, and I just jumped my highest."

Gators fans may argue about the loudest moment at The Swamp, but that blocked kick is definitely in the conversation. The players—both on the field and on the sideline—immediately ran to the corners of the end zone to celebrate with the fans. "It may be the Year of the Gator," Spurrier said after the game.

The coach was right.

Florida finished its regular season by winning for the second straight time in Tallahassee. By the time the Gators went to Atlanta to face Arkansas, they had moved to fourth in the BCS. Meyer had campaigned for his team after the FSU win, saying that No. 3 Michigan—which had lost to No. 1 Ohio State the week before—"had their shot." Florida would rally to beat Arkansas in the SEC Championship Game. On the same day, UCLA did the Gators a huge favor and knocked off No. 2 Southern Cal. When the final BCS standings came out the next day, Florida had leapfrogged Michigan and would play Ohio State for the national title.

# 13 Florida vs. the Girls School

The University of Florida is not lacking in its football rivalries. There's Tennessee, a rivalry made of conference alignment; the border rivalry that is Georgia; and then there is Florida State. Urban Meyer referred to it as the "school out West." Steve Spurrier called it "Free Shoes University." Some call it "the clown school" because FSU is one of the few universities with a circus. Gators fans call it a "girls school" based on the fact that it was one until 1947. By any name, there is no love lost between the two schools.

It goes back to the beginning when Florida State College for Women went coed and shortened its name to Florida State. Almost immediately there was a cry from Tallahassee for Florida to schedule a game with the new football program in the state. UF wanted no part of it because playing FSU would legitimize the fledgling program. The noises got louder, politicians got involved, and eventually the two school presidents were summoned by Governor LeRoy Collins to resolve the issue.

It was resolved, and the two football schools faced off for the first time in 1958 with Florida winning 21–7 behind 140-pound Jimmy Dunn, who scored twice on quarterback scrambles. Dunn had originally planned to be a Seminole but changed his mind when Florida offered a four-year scholarship. Florida dominated the rivalry early, winning the first six contests. FSU didn't get a win until 1964. Florida's players taped "Never FSU Never" on their practice helmets and stitched "Go For Seven" on their jerseys (although one of the previous six games was a tie).

The next year featured a hotly contested matchup when FSU's Lane Fenner caught what appeared to be a 45-yard touchdown pass with 17 seconds to go to give the Seminoles the win. But he was ruled out of bounds by field judge Doug Moseley, an SEC official. A year later when FSU played in Gainesville, one of the buses full of FSU fans had a still picture of Fenner's catch taped to its side.

Further intrigue would characterize the rivalry during the early 1980s. After a 1980 loss in Tallahassee, Florida coach Charley Pell told his team it would never lose to FSU again. And it didn't while Pell was the coach. In 1982 Florida won in Tallahassee, and Gator fans stormed the field until FSU officials turned on the sprinkler system.

The rivalry escalated in the 1990s when Bobby Bowden and Steve Spurrier were having great success at their respective schools. The two teams even played in a pair of Sugar Bowls following the 1994 and '96 seasons. The 1994 regular season had ended with the game that is referred to as "The Choke at Doak." Florida blew a 31–3 fourth-quarter lead as FSU roared back for a 31-all tie. (College football didn't have an overtime rule back then.) Sugar Bowl officials billed the matchup between the two teams as "The Fifth Quarter in the French Quarter." In '96 Spurrier accused the FSU players of hitting his quarterback Danny Wuerffel late. This was the same Spurrier who had taken to calling the FSU team "the Semis" instead of their preferred shortened nickname of the 'Noles. Florida beat FSU in New Orleans to win its first national title that same year.

A skirmish broke out before the 1998 game at midfield. Florida starting safety Tony George was ejected before the game ever started as was an injured FSU player. "We lost one of our best players," Spurrier said, "and they lost a guy in jeans." In 2001 Florida handled the Seminoles but lost tailback Earnest Graham to a knee injury. Spurrier accused FSU's Darnell Dockett of twisting Graham's knee while he was down, and Dockett bragged in the FSU locker room, "Did you see what I did to Earnest Graham?" Spurrier was so incensed by that incident and video, showing

Dockett trying to step on quarterback Rex Grossman's hand on the sideline, that Spurrier brought reporters to his office to show them footage of both incidents.

Then there was the "Swindle at The Swamp." In 2003, before instant replay, several questionable calls went FSU's way. Two Seminole fumbles were not called fumbles by the ACC crew. On two Florida fumbles, it appeared the runner was down, but they were ruled fumbles—at least that's the way Gator fans saw it. FSU won on a late touchdown. A year later during his final game as Florida coach, Ron Zook, who was fired during midseason, had his revenge, beating FSU in Tallahassee on the night they dedicated Bobby Bowden Field.

Meyer dominated the series, winning his first five tries against the Seminoles before losing in his final regular season game as Florida's coach. Just days after saying the program "needs fixing," Meyer stepped down as UF's coach. Will Muschamp's first effort against the Seminoles saw FSU win 21–7 despite gaining only 95 yards in the game. On his second try, Muschamp scored a big 37–26 win in Tallahassee to put Florida in position for the Sugar Bowl.

# 14 Steve Superior

Go ahead and ask him. Ask Steve Spurrier about a game he played in during his college career. Some players will give you vague answers about plays from almost 50 years ago. But Spurrier never forgets anything.

He remembers Florida being down 20–0 in the Sugar Bowl against Missouri following the 1965 season. "I came over to our

*Before becoming a coach, Steve Spurrier starred as the Florida quarterback and led the Gators to an Orange Bowl victory.*

offensive coordinator Ed Kensler and asked him what we should do,and he said, 'I don't know,'" Spurrier said. "So I said, 'Well, I better make up some plays.'" Or that classic 30–27 win against Auburn when the Tigers nearly won the game on a 91-yard fumble return by Gusty Yearout. "I started chasing him and [receiver] Richard Trapp sprinted past me," Spurrier said. "I yelled at him, 'Go get him, Dickie.'"

Spurrier remembers every play from every game he played in. He remembers baskets he made at Science Hill High in Johnson City, Tennessee, and he can give you the hole-by-hole breakdown of his best round of golf. It's that sharp mind that helped Spurrier become a great quarterback, but it was more than that. There was swagger, confidence, and talent.

Spurrier was a three-sport star at Science Hill where the football field is named for him. He had the will to win embedded in him by his father, Graham, a Presbyterian minister who pushed his son to never accept defeat. Spurrier might have been a better baseball player, never losing a game as a pitcher in three years, and he was an All-State basketball player, but according to Spurrier, "I wasn't going to quit football."

Most assumed Spurrier, who was recruited by the SEC's biggest schools, would end up at Tennessee. Alabama was also a possibility. But the Vols were running the single wing, and Spurrier wanted to fling it. Ray Graves wanted to throw it, too. He was ready to open up his offense at Florida and visited Spurrier in Johnson City several times. When Spurrier made his official visit to UF, he was suffering from a cold but liked that it was warm enough that he could get in a quick nine holes.

In his three years at Florida (freshmen were ineligible to play then), Spurrier didn't put up numbers that we would consider impressive today. In fact he threw for almost 7,000 fewer yards than Florida's all-time leader Chris Leak. And Spurrier never won an SEC Championship. Maybe that's what drove him to want to win so many as a coach. But Spurrier was a guy you couldn't stop watching and he found ways to win games. Spurrier passed, ran, kicked field goals on occasion, and was the team's punter. In his sophomore season, he split time with Tommy Shannon, but in the fourth quarter Spurrier was always the man.

When Florida trailed Mississippi State 13–3 in the fourth quarter in Jackson, Mississippi, Spurrier engineered a comeback and a 16–13 win. During his junior season, the Gators found themselves trailing Florida State 17–16 late in the game, and Spurrier drove the Gators to the winning touchdown. That play was vintage Spurrier. The quarterback knew he had a free play after an FSU player jumped offside. The play—94 block pass—was supposed to be an out to end Charlie Casey. But Spurrier waved Casey to cut up after running the out. "The corner ran right past me because he was going to jump the pass," Casey said. "I was all alone." That touchdown and Allen Trammell's interception return gave Florida an important 30–17 win.

Spurrier's legend grew as a senior when Auburn coach Shug Jordan mispronounced the quarterback's name as "Superior." Steve Superior stuck, and Spurrier kept winning games, including kicking a 40-yard field goal to beat Auburn. After that game, *The Gainesville Sun* sports editor Joe Halberstein wrote, "There's almost nothing left to say. Spurrier is fantastic when he has to be."

That game propelled Spurrier to Florida's first ever Heisman Trophy. In his final game of his college career, Spurrier helped UF stun Georgia Tech in the Orange Bowl. In his three years at Florida, the Gators went 23–9 and never won a title. But his play and that Heisman Trophy put the Gators on the national college football map.

# Charley Pell Lays the Foundation

Fans who walk into Ben Hill Griffin Stadium, tour the locker room, or meet with friends at a Gator Club probably wouldn't have recognized the Gator Nation before Charley Pell arrived in 1979. The facilities were awful—some of the worst in the SEC. There were no Gator Clubs. The stadium seated 70,000 and was rarely full.

Although Pell may be looked at as a villain because of the NCAA violations that cost him his job in 1984, he has to be remembered as the guy who set in motion many of the instruments that allowed Florida to become an elite college football program. "He wasn't afraid to go out and get with donors," said Phil Pharr, who was a center for Pell from 1980 to 1983 and is now the executive director of the Gator Boosters. "He was the guy who would sit down and say, 'This is what we have to do to make our program better.'"

Much of that involved raising money, and Pell became good friends with citrus magnate Ben Hill Griffin, who donated millions to the school and the football program. Pell also started the Gator Clubs around the state and eventually the country and made it a part of every assistant coach's job to attend the meetings and glad-hand with the fans. "He wanted us to be smarter with our efforts," Pharr said. "He was the guy who circled the wagons. We have to be unified." Pell raised money to have the weight room and locker rooms upgraded and pushed for expansion of the south end zone.

And the players he brought to Gainesville were pretty good, too. Pell's first team went 0–10–1, but he had the biggest turnaround (at the time) in college football history when he went 8–4 the following year. Pell emphasized socializing with the media, holding parties after games and golf tournaments in the summer. Always looking for an angle, he was a tireless recruiter. Unfortunately, his methods weren't always on the up and up.

Early in his tenure at Florida, Pell went to Florida sports information director John Humenik and asked for a glossy pamphlet that he would be able to give to potential recruits. It would include all kinds of information about the school, the program, the coaches, and the girls.

When Humenik finished the prototype, he handed it to Pell, who looked it over and approved. "Charley, we don't have room for this in our budget," Humenik said. "Who do I charge it to?" Pell took a long drag on his Vantage cigarette, looked up through the haze of smoke and said, "Charge it to winning."

# 16 Visit the Statues of the Heisman Winners

On the day that Florida played its annual Orange and Blue spring game, the pass that received the most cheers was not thrown by anyone who would play for the Gators the following fall.

And it was incomplete.

But when Tim Tebow walked from the visitors' entrance in the southeast corner of the stadium along the back line of the end zone, all eyes were diverted from the future to the past. An errant pass landed near Tebow. He picked it up and flung it back to the field of play where it landed harmlessly on the ground. The crowd went crazy, reacting as if he'd just thrown a touchdown pass.

Tebow had returned on this April 9, 2011 date because the University Athletic Association had statues ready to unveil. Florida coach Urban Meyer came up with the idea after the 2007 season when Tebow became the third Florida quarterback to win a Heisman Trophy. Meyer wanted to find a way to honor all three winners of the award.

Different ideas were bounced around before the bronze statues were approved by the UAA. Then the UAA found a great sculptor in W. Stanley "Sandy" Parker of Tallahassee. Parker had each of the subjects get plaster molds made of their faces and bodies to make sure the detail was there. Each of the statues weighs between 1,700 and 2,000 pounds and costs $550,000. Private donors gave the money to have the statues sculpted, and their names are on each of the statues. James W. "Bill" and Chase Heavener paid for the statues of Wuerffel and Tebow while Paul and Opal McDonald—on behalf of daughters Paula and Debra—deserve credit for the Spurrier statue.

There is room for more.

The statues were placed on the west side outside the stadium near the skybox entrance in a spot where there is space on each side. A palm tree or two might have to come down if Florida has another Heisman winner, but Gator Nation could make it work. For now the three will stand as the Gator representatives of college football's highest honor. Tebow is shown running the football, and Wuerffel and Spurrier are throwing it. "That's okay," Tebow said when the statues were unveiled. "They can't all be throwing."

When Florida unveiled the statues at halftime of the 2011 spring game, Spurrier could not be there because he was coaching South Carolina's spring game. His daughter Amy Moody, who lives in Panama City, Florida, subbed for the 1966 Heisman winner. "It's kind of hard to put in words," Moody said. "It's not often in life people dedicate a statue to you. It means a great deal."

But not all Gator fans were thrilled when Spurrier appeared on the video screen to give his speech. He was wearing a South Carolina golf shirt with a big South Carolina logo on the wall behind him. Less than six months earlier, Spurrier's Gamecocks had throttled Florida with the SEC East hanging in the balance. "This is one of the best honors I've had in my life," Spurrier said.

Wuerffel, like Tebow, returned to his alma mater for the honor. "When do you ever think growing up that you'll have a statue somewhere where people will look at it and have great memories?" Wuerffel said. "It's even more special being next to two guys that I love and admire in my coach, Steve Spurrier, and my friend, Tim Tebow. That even makes it more special for me." The statues have become not only a must-see for Gator fans—especially on gamedays—but thousands of fans have had their pictures taken next to the Tebow statue. They can only get so close as the area is cordoned off, and UF has a security guard there on game days.

# 17 The Super Sophs

It was another one of those years that had failed to live up to its promise. Injuries to Larry Smith and fumbles at North Carolina had turned 1968 into another epic fail for "The Year of the Gator." For once the tired cry of, "Wait 'Til Next Year," had some merit. Florida had a group of freshmen who were about to explode on the scene. There were signs of it in '68 when the newbies were playing against other freshmen teams and even against their varsity brethren.

One of the low points during the era coached by Ray Graves was a 51–0 loss in the rain against Georgia. But later that week the freshmen went to Athens, Georgia, and beat the Bulldogs. "It was snowing, too," wide receiver Carlos Alvarez said. "It meant a lot to us to go up there and do that after what they had done to the varsity."

In the spring game, the young guys beat the veterans 48–6. In a scrimmage against the second team, they scored 93 points. "That's when coaches knew we might have something here," quarterback John Reaves said. Reaves, Alvarez, tailback Tommy "Touchdown" Durrance, and fullback Mike Rich were the all-sophomore backfield that was nicknamed the "Super Sophs." They had plenty of veteran help, including two running backs in Jerry Vinesett and Gary Walker, and an offensive line loaded with veterans. But the Reaves-to-Alvarez combination brought the ability to stretch the field to Florida. And it didn't take long for Gator fans to find out.

The opener in 1969 was at home against Houston, a team that had been selected as the nation's No. 1 team by *Playboy* and scored 100 points in a game the year before. On the third play of the game, Reaves called for 79 streak, dropped back, and hit Alvarez alone deep down the field, and Alvarez took it in for a 74-yard touchdown. "He was five yards behind the guy," Reaves said. "And they weren't going to catch him." Alvarez, a Cuban immigrant who had to learn English from classmates at school, was one of the fastest players in the country until he hurt his knee after his sophomore season running track. He earned his own nickname, "the Cuban Comet."

Florida kept piling up the points. As a result, fans, who had been listening to the game, began heading for Florida Field. UF sold almost as many tickets at halftime as it did pregame. Florida went on to win the game 59–34 and went from unranked to No. 12 in the Associated Press poll. The next week they scored 47 points against Mississippi State and went on to score 52 against North Carolina and 41 against Vanderbilt. Even when the offense struggled against Tulane, Florida managed a two-point conversion to pull out an 18–17 win.

It all came crashing down when Reaves threw nine interceptions—a record that probably will never be topped—in a 38–12 loss to Auburn. The Gators tied hated Georgia 13–13 the following week when a late field goal try was botched. But these Gators were invited to the Gator Bowl.

They, however, didn't know that Graves had been pressured before the season to resign as head coach and just serve as athletic director. When the 1969 team had so much success, Graves wanted to stay as coach, but UF officials already began negotiating with Tennessee coach Doug Dickey. Ironically, Tennessee was Florida's opponent in the Gator Bowl.

Florida won 14–13 on a touchdown pass from Reaves to Alvarez, and a few days later, Dickey was named the new coach. The players were incensed and Alvarez, now a lawyer in Tallahassee, Florida, tried to start a players union on campus and demanded that the players have a say in the hiring and firing of coaches. Alvarez is the only one of the Super Sophs to be inducted into the College Football Hall of Fame. Durrance, whose single-season record of 18 touchdowns in '69 lasted until Reidel Anthony tied it in 1996 and Tim Tebow broke it with 23 in 2007, passed away in 2005 after a battle with brain cancer.

# 18 Ike and Reidel

During the three seasons Ike Hilliard and Reidel Anthony played together at Florida, you almost could not say one name without the other. Ike and Reidel were the primary targets for Terry Dean and then for Danny Wuerffel, and the wide receiver pair helped Florida win three straight SEC titles and reach two national title games.

The two men came from different parts of the country— Anthony from the impoverished Belle Glades area in South Florida and Hilliard from Patterson, Louisiana. "I played free safety and running back in a wishbone offense," Hilliard said. "But I told anybody who came in I wanted to play wide receiver. I weighed 171 pounds and I was looking at running backs like Jerome Bettis and Natrone Means and I didn't want any part of that. LSU didn't recruit me as a receiver. A lot of schools didn't because I didn't have any wide receiver film. They didn't appreciate that I didn't want to play defensive back. Coach [Steve] Spurrier said they already had the five guys they wanted. But he said I was a good enough athlete [that] he'd give me a shot."

Anthony was part of a powerful Belle Glades Central team that included another player who would be part of that class, running back Fred Taylor. Some people thought it was a package deal—that Florida recruited the skinny Anthony to help lure Taylor and Glades Central linebacker Johnny Rutledge to UF. But Anthony was perfect a fit in Spurrier's Fun 'n' Gun offense. He had speed and soft hands and wasn't afraid to go up and get the ball. Sometimes it looked as if he was climbing a ladder to reach a high pass.

Hilliard was smoother and had the advantage of sometimes getting matched up against a linebacker when Florida went to four wide receivers. Both players shined when the lights were the brightest. Hilliard had four touchdowns in a comeback win against Tennessee in 1995 and three when Florida won the national title. Anthony had three touchdown catches when the Gators won the 1996 SEC Championship against Alabama.

Perhaps the best Anthony moment cane on a rainy day in Auburn, Alabama, in 1995. Florida had lost two in a row to Terry Bowden's Tigers, and the game started with Wuerffel losing a fumble and throwing an interception. As he came off the field, Spurrier said to his quarterback, "Danny, are you trying to lose the game all by yourself?" Up 10–0 after the turnovers, Auburn kicked off to Anthony, and he raced 90 yards, making one cut that froze a defender and scored a touchdown that totally changed the momentum of the game.

Florida had other targets during those three years, most notably Jacquez Green, but it was the Ike and Reidel Show for the most part. Just look how similar their final stats were: Anthony had 126 catches, 2,274 yards, and 26 touchdowns, and Hilliard had 126 catches, 2,214 yards, and 29 touchdowns. Both left Florida after their junior seasons and both were first-round picks.

# 19 Emmitt Smith

There was a time when National Signing Day wasn't that big a deal. Colleges around the country would recruit high school football players and quietly announce their class. If you want to point to an event where that changed—where recruiting analysis went from a cottage industry to a national phenomenon—it was the day Emmitt Smith signed with Florida.

Heavily recruited out of Pensacola Escambia High, Smith's final two schools were supposed to be Auburn and Nebraska, two programs that featured power running games. On National Signing Day, Smith showed up wearing red and white clothes. He had told friends that the colors he wore would indicate where he would go. So it certainly looked like Nebraska. After several Escambia players signed with major colleges that afternoon, Smith went last and announced that he would sign with Florida.

A recruiting analyst, Max Emfinger, called Smith "a lugger, not a runner," But boy, could Smith run. Florida coach Galen Hall wanted to ease him into the lineup. He barely played in a loss at

*Florida freshman running back Emmitt Smith eludes Ben Hummel (45) and the rest of the UCLA defense during the 1987 Aloha Bowl.* (AP Images)

Miami and carried only 10 times in the second game of the season against Tulsa. One of those carries produced a 66-yard touchdown run, and Smith started the next week.

Florida went to Birmingham, Alabama, to face the No. 11 Alabama Crimson Tide. Hall decided to lean heavily on Smith and he bolstered a shaky offensive line by having 230-pound fullback Willie McGrady lead the way when Smith carried the ball. Smith responded in a big way. He rushed for 224 yards, an SEC record for a freshman, as Florida surprised Alabama 23–14. The headline in *The Gainesville Sun* the next day read: "Freshman Rush." Smith went on to become the SEC Freshman of the Year, even though Florida faded down the stretch, losing four of its last five games, including a Hula Bowl loss to UCLA and Troy Aikman, Smith's future teammate on the Dallas Cowboys.

The Gators started out the next season by winning their first five games behind Smith. But in the sixth game, Smith was lost to a knee injury, and quarterback Kyle Morris injured his throwing hand on the final play of an upset loss against Memphis State. Smith missed the next three games, and Florida's season turned into a grease fire. The Gators lost five of their last six games. They, though, did receive an invitation to the Hall of Fame Bowl in Birmingham, Alabama, where Smith had first burst onto the college football scene. This time he needed only one play to make some noise. On Florida's first offensive play of the game, Smith ran 55 yards for a touchdown. Florida salvaged a winning record with a 14–10 victory against Illinois and quarterback Jeff George.

By Smith's junior season, things were falling apart at UF. The NCAA was deep into an investigation of the basketball program that leaked into football. Five games into the season, Hall was forced to resign because of NCAA violations. A little more than a week later, Morris and three backup players was suspended for placing bets with a bookie in Athens, Georgia. But before the 1989 season went off the cliff, Smith did everything he could to put the

## Emmitt's Records

When Emmitt Smith left Florida after three seasons, he held 58 school marks, but records are made to be broken, and some of his were. Here's where he stands in several Florida Gators categories.

**Career rushing attempts**—Smith ranks second with 700. Errict Rhett, who played four seasons, has the record with 873.

**Career rushing yards**—Smith ranks second with 3,928. Rhett also has this record with 4,163 yards.

**Career yards per game**—Smith owns this record at 126.7 yards.

**Single-season rushing yards**—This mark still belongs to Smith at 1,599 yards in 1989.

**Career rushing touchdowns rushing**—Smith ranks second with 36. Tim Tebow shattered the record with 57.

**Career 100-yard rushing games**—Smith owns this record with 23, including a record six straight.

**Longest run from scrimmage**—Smith owns this mark. He ran for 96 yards on a run up the middle against Mississippi State in 1988.

team on his back. In a homecoming win over New Mexico, he rushed for a school-record 316 yards. Under interim head coach Gary Darnell, Florida rarely threw the ball and instead leaned on Smith. That strategy almost worked in Auburn, Alabama, but a late Tigers touchdown broke the hearts of a team that had been through so much. Florida lost by a touchdown the following week against Georgia and by a touchdown at the end of the regular season to FSU. Florida went to the Freedom Bowl in Anaheim, California, where Smith carried the ball seven times, took his pads off at half-time, and signed autographs the rest of the game.

It was a bizarre way for one of the greatest players in Florida history to end his career. When Steve Spurrier came in to coach the Gators the following year, Smith decided to bolt for the NFL. Spurrier wasn't one to beg a player to stay, and Smith felt the new coach could have tried a little harder to convince him to stick around.

Selected with the 17th pick in the first round of the 1990 NFL Draft by Dallas, Smith went on to become the NFL's all-time rushing leader. His relationship with the school ran hot and cold, and when he was inducted into the Pro Football Hall of Fame in 2010 and didn't mention UF, there was an assumption that it had to do with his feelings about Spurrier. In truth Smith's original acceptance speech ran 30 minutes long, and he was told to cut it, and he accidentally forgot to thank Florida. Smith apologized profusely on *Monday Night Football* and Twitter for the alleged snub of his alma mater.

# 20 The World's Largest Outdoor Cocktail Party

When Florida and Georgia decided to start playing their annual football game in Jacksonville, Florida, starting in 1933, officials on both sides probably had little idea what a spectacle it would become.

The teams had played at neutral sites such as Tampa, Florida, and Savannah, Georgia, as well as Jacksonville prior to '33. Once it landed in Jacksonville, it would move only twice. In 1994 (Gainesville) and 1995 (Athens), the game was played on the campuses because of renovations to the Gator Bowl for the incoming NFL team—the Jacksonville Jaguars.

Florida and Georgia are natural rivals because the states border each other, and they are both in the SEC (and the SEC East as of 1992). The rivalry has extended to the record books where Georgia claims a win in 1904 that Florida does not acknowledge because UF claims it started football in 1906. The intensity has been impassioned on and off the field. With half the crowd from Georgia and half from Florida, there are more opportunities for heated interaction between opposing fans.

In 1992 after Florida's third straight win, *The Atlanta Journal Constitution* columnist Lewis Grizzard wrote that the game should leave Jacksonville. "It's the World's Largest Crazy House," he wrote. Grizzard had some bad experiences in Jacksonville. In the 1970s he and fellow *AJC* columnist Furman Bisher were denied access to press parking despite having passes. They left their rental car running in the street to make the game in time. And Grizzard wasn't the only person to push for the game to move. In 1985 there were concerns about the state of the Gator Bowl. In 2009 Georgia coach Mark Richt suggested the game move to the Georgia Dome every fourth year. But each time Jacksonville has come through to meet the demands of both schools because of the economic impact (estimated to be around $80 million) on the city and surrounding areas. From Jekyll Island, Georgia, in the north to St. Augustine, Florida, in the south, the hotels and restaurants fill up with fans, who use the game as a reason for a long weekend vacation. Recreational vehicles start lining up for parking on Tuesday of game week, and the party takes place more during the week than on Saturday.

But the nickname—The World's Largest Outdoor Cocktail Party—goes back to one incident in the 1950s. *The Florida Times-Union* columnist Bill Kastelz saw an inebriated fan offer an alcoholic beverage to an on-duty cop and came up with the moniker. It stuck until the presidents of the two schools asked fans, media, and CBS (which broadcast the game) to drop it in 2006. In 2004 and '05, a UF student died after each game. One fell from the roof of a parking garage; the other was beaten to death.

The WLOCP moniker is still used, but it is not as prevalent as it was prior to 2006. The decline in use, though, has not stopped the party. In 2012 an inebriated fan was sent to the hospital after a fight in one of the parking lots' retention ponds.

Even with the issues and the traffic, there are two reasons why the game is booked through 2016 and isn't likely to go anywhere. And they both involve math. The two schools receive approximately $1.7 million a year from the city and through ticket sales (with 10,000 bleacher seats added for the game each year). If the game went home and home, each school would make more than a million dollars less for each two-year span.

Reason No. 2 is that boosters who get tickets for the game would have more trouble acquiring tickets. Contracts with SEC schools usually require only 10 percent of the tickets be available to the visitors. That would be around 9,000 for Florida fans when the game is at Athens. That's far short of the 40,000 that are available now.

# 21 Kerwin's Comeback

Galen Hall sat in the skybox at Florida Field, sipping on a cold beer two hours after the final whistle had sounded on one of the greatest comebacks in Florida history. (This was back in 1986 when the coach at Florida would play host to an after-party for the media once they had finished their stories.) Hall was asked about the play, the one that had resulted in an 18–17 victory against Auburn. "Well, we told Kerwin [Bell] to roll right," Hall deadpanned, "and then run around and score."

It was hardly that simple and even more improbable. A quarterback who wasn't supposed to play would cap an amazing comeback by running in a two-point conversion. Bell had a torn meniscus in his knee that had kept him out of the previous two games. "It was hurting, and they had me in a big brace that felt like it really slowed me down," Bell said. "Not that I was all that fast to begin with." Hall told Bell he'd dress for the game but would only play in an emergency. Auburn was unbeaten, ranked fifth, and sported a ferocious defense led by Aundray Bruce, who would become the first overall pick in the 1988 NFL Draft. That defense forced Florida quarterback Rodney Brewer into four turnovers in the first half. With Florida trailing 17–0, Hall inserted Bell into the game.

The former walk-on had once been listed eighth on the quarterback depth chart but moved up to Opening Day starter in 1984 when others ahead of him either moved to another position or were injured. A native of tiny Mayo, Florida, he earned the nickname "the Throwin' Mayoan" during the 1984 season when Florida was good enough to win the SEC title. That title was later stripped, and the Gators were ruled ineligible in 1985 when they again had the league's best record. But by 1986 the scholarship reductions that accompanied the NCAA penalties against Florida were beginning to hinder the Gators. "We had guys playing that shouldn't even have been on scholarship," Bell said.

After an opening win, Florida lost four straight games. In the loss to LSU, Bell suffered the injury and missed wins against Kent State and Rutgers. But when Brewer struggled against the Auburn pass rush, Hall felt he had to go with his injured quarterback. "I wasn't sure I wanted to go in," Bell said. "Auburn was that good on defense."

It didn't go well for Bell either…at first. Struggling with the brace and the pain in his left knee, Bell—throwing an interception on his first pass attempt—and the Gators failed to get anything going until the second half. Finally a 79-yard scoring drive was capped by Bell's quarterback sneak for a touchdown early in the fourth quarter. Then another drive ended when Robert McGinty kicked a 51-yard field goal. In a delicious bit of revenge, McGinty had transferred from Auburn to Florida because Auburn coach Pat Dye would not give him a scholarship. McGinty's field goal was his first since the last game of the 1984 season when he missed a game-winner against Alabama.

Down 17–10 Florida's defense needed a stop, but Auburn's star tailback, Brent Fullwood, was running out the clock. However, Auburn fullback Reggie Ware fumbled on the Florida 34-yard line, giving the Gators hope with 1:41 left in the game. Auburn sacked Bell on the first play and received a facemask penalty. "That gave us life," Bell said.

Somehow Bell scrambled away from the Auburn rush to complete a pass to Darrell Woulard, who ran to the Auburn 21-yard line. The Gators caught another break when Woulard fumbled out of bounds, stopping the clock. On the next play, Bell hit wide receiver Ricky Nattiel to get to the Auburn 5-yard line. Nattiel had suffered a separated left shoulder in the third quarter but—like Bell—was playing through the pain. With only 36 seconds to play, Nattiel ran a fade route from the slot, and Bell found him in the end zone with a perfectly thrown pass. Hall decided to go for two. "I just wanted to get out of there with the tie," Bell said.

The play called for Bell to roll right, but nothing was open. He planted, eluded Auburn defensive end Tracy Rocker, and began running toward the left. He sprinted to the goal line, diving in as he was hit by two Auburn defenders. As Bell rose to his knees, he was crushed in celebration by offensive lineman Bob Sims. Florida fans who had been suffering through a miserable season celebrated like they had just won a national title.

Florida carried the momentum of the win into Jacksonville, Florida, where it beat Georgia. Despite their 6–5 record, the Gators were not offered a bowl trip at the end of the season.

# 22 The Great Wall of Florida

Most of them would be considered undersized today. But in 1984 they were giants.

The five players who made up the offensive line for the '84 Gators were so good they were given their own nickname—"the Great Wall of Florida." They were considered impenetrable to pass rushers while blowing open holes for Florida's talented running backs during a 9–1–1 season. Florida led the SEC in scoring and averaged five yards per rushing attempt.

Nobody had a better view of the line than the team's redshirt freshman quarterback Kerwin Bell. And nobody appreciated it more. "It was the best year I ever had," Bell said. "I didn't get touched. I think I only got sacked seven times all season. The pass protection was as good as it gets."

The line was made up of four seniors and redshirt freshman Jeff Zimmerman, who was easily the biggest of the linemen at 330 pounds. "You didn't see that back in the '80s," Bell said. "A 300-plus pounder coming out of high school? We couldn't find a helmet that fit him."

Here is Bell's view of Zimmerman and the other four players who made up "The Great Wall of Florida." Center Phil Bromley: "He was real small for a center [240 pounds], but he was so smart. He had a lot of experience and he was the guy that I remember kind of held that line together. He was very quick and athletic." Guards Zimmerman and Billy Hinson: "They were two big burly guys that we used to call the load-graders. They had great movement and were excellent run blockers." Tackles Lomas Brown and Crawford Ker: "Crawford's nickname was 'Big Daddy,' and he went about

290 pounds. He had come out of high school at about 200 pounds, an undersized defensive lineman. And he went to junior college and showed up back at Florida at 290. Both of the tackles were extremely athletic. Lomas was as good a tackle as you'll see, and Big Daddy at right tackle was really good as well."

Three members of the Great Wall went on to play in the NFL—Brown, Zimmerman, and Ker, who now owns a national chain of restaurants called Ker's Wing House. "What was real special for that line was that all five of them could bench press over 400 pounds," Bell said. "And that was rare at the time."

It was Ker, according to longtime UF sports information director Norm Carlson, who came up with the moniker. "He said, 'We're a bunch of big guys forming this Great Wall,'" Carlson said. "It was such a great name we went with it and started using it, and it caught on, and the media started using it."

# 23 Jack Youngblood

It's difficult to believe that a guy who would eventually receive induction into the Pro Football Hall of Fame and Florida's Ring of Honor would have as many offers during his senior year of high school as the team's waterboy. But the interest in Jack Youngblood during his state championship season at Monticello, Florida's Jefferson County High was zilch, nada, nil. He had no offers. Florida State assistant coach Bill Parcells had scouted him and decided he couldn't play at the next level.

One issue was that nobody could figure out what to do with him. Youngblood had dealt with problems in his legs—one grew faster than the other—and had to sit out games because of the pain. He had grown to 6'4", but there wasn't a lot of meat on the frame for a guy who was playing middle linebacker. "I had to run around in the shower to get wet," he said.

Youngblood planned to attend North Florida Junior College and figure out what he wanted to do with his life. Celebrating with his teammates after they won the Florida Class B championship in his senior year, Youngblood was approached by Dave Fuller, Florida's baseball coach, and recruited for the football team. He had been so impressed with the effort that he had seen out of Youngblood that he offered him a scholarship on the spot.

It took Youngblood a split second to accept. He shifted to defensive end at Florida and became an All-American. Each year he added weight through nutrition and weightlifting and eventually left Florida at 245 pounds. It was still small for a defensive end, but Youngblood had amazing quickness and the ability to strip the ball from running backs.

It was one of those strips that served as his most famous play at Florida. At the end of the third quarter, the Gators trailed Georgia 17–10 with Georgia on the Florida 1-yard line. On the first play of the fourth quarter, Youngblood ripped the ball away from Bulldog ball carrier Ricky Lake and recovered the ball himself. "It was just sitting there," he said. "So I jumped on it." Florida went down the field to tie the game and then won it on the next possession.

Youngblood was known for coming up with his best games when the lights were the brightest. He had nine tackles and a forced fumble against Tennessee in the 1969 Gator Bowl to boost the Gators to nine wins. He had five sacks during that season's game against FSU. Before going on to a 14-year career with the Los Angeles Rams, Youngblood was voted the SEC's Lineman of the Year.

He's best known for playing a Super Bowl game against Pittsburgh with a broken leg. But despite recording 151.5 sacks during his NFL career, it took Youngblood longer than usual to get into the NFL Hall of Fame. (He retired in 1985 but wasn't voted in until 2001.) Since the NFL didn't start to count sacks officially until 1982, some committee members refused to take all of his previous takedowns into account.

Youngblood eventually became Florida's first member of the Pro Football Hall of Fame and gave a memorable speech where he thanked the man who first offered him a scholarship. "There was a baseball coach at the University of Florida many years ago," Youngblood said as he stood before the crowd in Canton, Ohio. "He was scouting our territory and he saw a young man playing football in 1966. And he saw something in a young man playing the game that nobody else noticed. Coach Dave Fuller—he's smiling right now. He's not with us anymore either. But I want to thank coach Graves—coach Ray Graves—who was my football coach at the University of Florida for believing in a wise man, coach Dave Fuller. He saw a potential in a football player, and they made me a Gator. Not just for four years, but they made me a Gator for life."

The only trouble with his oration—Dave Fuller, who passed away in 2009, was still alive and living in Gainesville at the time of Youngblood's speech.

# 24 The Swamp

For weeks they had been trying to force a nickname on the stadium. Steve Spurrier, then the coach at Florida, and Norm Carlson, the sports information director, had been friends since Spurrier was

*Ben Hill Griffin Stadium is better known as "The Swamp," a nickname Steve Spurrier helped coin.*

a player at UF, and they spent a lot of time together in Crescent Beach in nearby St. Augustine, Florida. They would sit and try to come up with the perfect name for Ben Hill Griffin Stadium. For the most part, it was an epic fail. "Steve was big on nicknames and he felt like we needed one for the stadium," Carlson said. "We came up with some that were really stupid—The Gator Pit, The Gator Chomp, stuff like that."

Finally in October of 1992, Spurrier and Carlson were in the bowels of the stadium. Carlson started to tell Spurrier a story about how Florida Field was built. The Gators had been playing their games at Fleming Field, which is now a parking area north of the stadium. John Tigert, the president of the university, decided in 1930 that the football team needed a stadium. He picked out the site but needed to dry it out first. "I was telling Steve how Tigert had to cap active springs that are still there under the field and drain the water down to form what is now Graham Pond," Carlson said. "They had to drain the swamp and muck that was sitting there. And Steve said, 'Swampy. Swamp.' And we both looked at each other and said, 'The Swamp.' He kept saying it over and over. He loved it. And then he said, 'Only Gators get out alive.'"

Spurrier liked it so much he called Mike Bianchi, who was the columnist at *The Gainesville Sun*, to announce the new nickname for the stadium. Bianchi, a fan of nicknames himself who coined the term "Fun 'n' Gun" for Spurrier's offense, ran with it.

But not everyone was enamored with the name. When Spurrier took it to Florida's marketing department, he was told it would never catch on. Instead it became one of the most recognizable stadium names in all of sports. It helped that Spurrier's teams went 68–5 in The Swamp. The stadium has been through plenty of changes through the years. The first game was played on October 27, 1930 with a capacity crowd of 21,769. Since then:

- It was expanded by 11,200 seats in 1950.
- It was expanded again by another 10,000 seats in 1966.
- Artificial turf was installed in 1971 then ripped out for natural grass in 1990.
- The bleachers in the south end zone were replaced by permanent seating in 1982, bringing capacity to 72,000.
- The new north end zone was completed in 1991 to bring the capacity to 83,000, including skyboxes.
- A two-year project that cost $50 million added the Champions Club, moved the press box to the southwestern corner of the stadium, and pushed the capacity over 90,000 in 1993.

## Largest Swamp Crowds

1. **90,907**—November 28, 2009 vs. Florida State—Tim Tebow's last home game as a Gator
2. **90,894**—September 19, 2009 vs. Tennessee—Lane Kiffin's antics had Gator fans rabid.
3. **90,888**—October 1, 2011 vs. Alabama—UF takes on No. 3 and eventual national champion Tide.
4. **90,885**—November 13, 2010 vs. South Carolina—Spurrier returns with the SEC East title on the line.
5. **90,833**—September 6, 2008 vs. Miami—Miami's first visit since 2002
6. **90,798**—November 26, 2011 vs. Florida State—Rivalry is a big deal, even though neither team was ranked.
7. **90,744**—September 17, 2011 vs. Tennessee—Will Muschamp's first SEC game as Gators head coach
8. **90,721**—October 9, 2010 vs. LSU—Game matched two Top 15 teams.
9. **90,716**—September 17, 2005 vs. Tennessee—Urban Meyer's first SEC game as Gators head coach
10. **90,714**—October 7, 2006 vs. LSU—Game matched two Top 10 teams.

The stadium has also been through several facelifts to add to the aesthetic quality of the facility. In 2008 large banners were placed on the west side entrances of the stadium to honor some of the best players and teams in Gator history, and the same was done inside the stadium prior to the 2012 season. Inside the stadium the four orange walls at the corners carry slogans such as, "This Is... Gator Country," and, "Home Of...The Florida Gators."

The Ring of Honor rises into the sky above the north wall, and the Heisman Trophy winners are honored at the top of the south wall. Florida's national championship and SEC championship seasons are painted on the wall between the upper and lower decks in the south end zone.

Florida started doing that when the Gators won the national championship in 1996, but Spurrier felt strongly that his 1990 team belonged up there. That team would have won the SEC, but Florida was on probation because of the violations by previous coaching staff. But if he wanted 1990, that meant that 1984 and 1985, two other successful years while on probation, had to go up as well with "Best in the SEC" next to them.

A little more than a year after Spurrier left for the NFL, Florida removed those seasons from the wall.

# 25 Eat Lunch at The Other Swamp

Ron DeFilippo was walking to a Florida football game when he passed a place called Chaucer's. A former UF professor's home, the breakfast cafe had an ideal location across the street from campus and only a couple hundred yards from the stadium where the Gators played football. "There were these girls in pigtails outside selling chocolate chip cookies," he said. "I remember thinking that they were missing their market."

The building burned down in 1992 and remained boarded up until DeFilippo, a former UF journalism student, rented the land in 1994 and built a restaurant on the site. By then Steve Spurrier had named the stadium across the street. So DeFilippo figured the perfect name for it would be "The Swamp." "I should have trademarked it," he said. "Florida did trademark it later, but they said I just have to refer to my place and everything about it as 'The Swamp Restaurant,' which is fine."

The design of the restaurant has two stories with an open middle extending to the ceiling. Customers can dine on the patio upstairs, and there is an open front yard where people can enjoy the great Gainesville weather while eating lunch or watching a game on a big screen TV. DeFilippo also arranged for music to be played inside his white picket fence that borders University Avenue. Ken Block and Drew Copeland, who went on to form the band Sister Hazel, cut their teeth playing acoustic sets at The Swamp.

The restaurant opened briefly—for just one day to be exact—in 1994. Virginia Tech and Tennessee were playing the Gator Bowl game in Gainesville because of construction at Jacksonville, Florida's Gator Bowl, and DeFilippo had a buddy from Virginia Tech. So they opened The Swamp to the Hokies fans and even had the marching band playing on a side street. The restaurant officially opened in 1995 and struggled at first until DeFilippo brought some new chefs in to upgrade the menu. While burgers are still available, The Swamp's menu rotates meals on and off to keep it fresh and can include Hawaiian pork quesadillas, Cajun gator tail sliders, and beef tenderloin sandwiches. The walls of the place act as a museum to Gator greats. There are dozens of signed jerseys from UF athletes hanging on the walls as well as signed posters and memorabilia from past Gator games. "The timing was really good for us because we opened, and then so many great things happened for the Gators," DeFilippo said. "They started winning national championships, and people wanted to be here with their friends to celebrate. And the players—they just want to give us stuff all the time, so we try to rotate what we put up and try to keep it current."

Because many of Florida's sports teams play within walking distance, The Swamp is an ideal meeting spot for Gators fans before games. A place for Florida players to celebrate big victories, it's not unusual to bump into the player who made the winning shot in a hoops game. Former UF quarterback John Brantley would meet his father, John Sr., at The Swamp for Thursday night dinner before every one of his starts. National radio and television shows have broadcast live from the outdoor patio. "It's a real success story," DeFilippo said. "People come here as freshmen, and the next thing you know we're getting wedding invitations from them in the mail. It's really become a landmark for the students."

# The First SEC Championship Game

It was a brainchild of Roy Kramer, the innovative SEC commissioner from 1990 to 2002. Only seven months after he became commissioner, Kramer was welcoming two new schools to the conference, which allowed the SEC to do what it really wanted. An NCAA bylaw allows a conference with 12 members to split into divisions and hold a conference championship game at the end of the regular season. That was part of the thinking in adding South Carolina and Arkansas for the 1992 season.

The conference title game would bring major revenue both in tickets sales and licensing to the football-crazy conference. The first game was played at Legion Field in Birmingham, Alabama, where the SEC offices are located. Alabama cruised into the game. Florida backed its way in. "The scholarship reductions [from 1990] had really affected our team," quarterback Shane Matthews said.

Matthews was a senior, but he was running for his life behind an offensive line that included two true freshmen tackles in Reggie Green and Jason Odom. Florida lost at Tennessee in Week Two and then was humiliated 30–6 at Mississippi State in the only ESPN Thursday night game the Gators have ever played. But somehow the Gators won their next seven games, and Tennessee fumbled away an opportunity to win the newly formed SEC East. Florida had worked itself all the way up to sixth in the rankings before its annual game against Florida State. Spurrier was so intent on winning the SEC championship that he pulled Matthews at halftime of the FSU game to ensure his quarterback would be healthy the following week against Alabama.

The Tide came in ranked second in the country and as a 10-point favorite. Not only was Alabama trying to reach a national title game, the Tide was basically playing in front of a home crowd. "We were certainly looking forward to the game," Spurrier said. "We knew if we could win it wouldn't only mean the SEC title, but it would have been one of the biggest upsets in Florida history and maybe in Alabama history."

Florida made the Alabama fans nervous when the Gators drove to score and take the lead. Spurrier had inserted a new play into the game plan where Matthews would drop back with the ball up around his chin and then whip it forward like a softball to running back Errict Rhett. Basically it was just another way to run a draw play. "It certainly negated their pass rush," Spurrier said.

Still Alabama's talent was too much for Florida in the second and third quarters as the Tide jumped out to a 21–7 lead. But Florida battled back, using a Matthews-to-Willie Jackson touchdown pass for one score and a 1-yard run by Rhett to tie the game with 8:01 to play. When the Gators got the ball back with just more than three minutes to play, the upset seemed not only possible but probable. But on the first play of Florida's drive, Matthews tried to hit receiver Monty Duncan on a short pass, and Alabama cornerback Antonio Langham stepped in front of the throw. He took it 21 yards for a score with 3:16 to play, and Florida couldn't do anything on its next possession, which ended with another interception. "Unfortunately, that's the game I remember the most in my career," Matthews said.

Spurrier had his quarterback's back. He called several media publications the following week to tell them that Duncan had run the wrong route, and that the pass wasn't Matthews' fault. Alabama would go on to beat Miami for the national title. The SEC championship would be played once more at Legion Field before it moved to Atlanta's Georgia Dome in 1994. The game would represent a huge success for the league, and the two schools, Florida and Alabama, would make the most appearances.

# 27 Tebow's Heisman Year

A group of reporters approached Urban Meyer just days before the spring game. They had been on the road following the Florida basketball team's run to a second straight national title and wanted to know how things were going with the football team back in Gainesville. One of them finally asked Meyer, "What's it like to have a quarterback get so much publicity who has never started a game?'

Meyer just laughed off the question. Tim Tebow had been a highly recruited quarterback and an important part in Florida's run to the 2006 national championship. But in 2007 he would get his first start for the Gators. Chris Leak had graduated, and it was the Tebow show now. All eyes were on a player who had already become a fan favorite for his ruggedness and enthusiasm on the field. But nobody was including Tebow on their Heisman Trophy watch lists. After all no sophomore had ever won the coveted award.

Tebow was about to make history.

It started with the opener against Western Kentucky when he scored the game's first touchdown from a yard out. He would also throw for three touchdowns against the Hilltoppers. (An interesting sidebar: the final Florida score came on a run by future Heisman winner Cam Newton.)

## Tebow's UF records

During Tim Tebow's four-year career at Florida, he set numerous UF records. Here are some of the ones that still stand:

**Career rushing touchdowns**—57
**Rushing yards by a quarterback**—2,947
**Career completion percentage**—66.4 percent
**Career passing efficiency rating**—170.79
**Consecutive passes without an interception**—203 (2007 to 2008)
**Total offense in a career**—12,352
**Total offense in a season**—4,181 (2007)
**Total touchdowns in a career**—145
**Total touchdowns in a season**—55 (2007)

Two weeks later during Tebow's first SEC start, the Gators put up 59 points for the second straight week as the sophomore ran for two scores and threw for two more. Tebow beating teams with his legs and his arm would become a season-long theme. To escape Ole Miss with a win a week later, Meyer put the ball in his quarterback's hands down the stretch, and Tebow set a school record for rushes by a quarterback with 27. "I'm not tired," said Tebow despite rushing for 166 yards.

Florida was shut out in the first half against Auburn as offensive coordinator Dan Mullen missed most of the week with an emergency appendectomy. Tebow rallied the Gators with a touchdown pass and a scoring run to tie the game, but the Tigers won on a late field goal.

LSU beat Florida the following week. Tebow accounted for three scores, but the young Gators defense couldn't get off the field in a 28–24 loss.

Tebow threw for four touchdowns in a win at Kentucky, but Florida's shot at the SEC title was lost against Georgia when the Bulldogs sacked Tebow six times. Despite the incredible numbers the quarterback had compiled, he was a dark horse Heisman contender because Florida had three losses. But five touchdowns against Vanderbilt unofficially cemented his candidacy.

Then came South Carolina.

Word began to circulate in the media and among the fans that star wide receiver Percy Harvin did not make the trip because of migraine headaches. Would Florida have enough offense to beat Steve Spurrier's team especially since the Gators defense had struggled so mightily?

Tebow had the answer. Florida won 51–31 as Tebow threw for a pair of scores and ran for five touchdowns. During his postgame press conference, Spurrier put on his reading glasses and checked out the stats. "I thought we talked about not letting him run it in there," Spurrier said. "How many did he run in? Two? Three?"

It was five.

"He ran for *five*?" Spurrier asked with an air of disbelief. "I guess I lost count."

The South Carolina game might have been the one that won Tebow the Heisman, but he backed it up the following week against Florida State. Early in the game, he dropped back to pass, made an incredible play to duck a pass rusher, and sprinted 23 yards for a touchdown. Near the goal line, he threw a stiff-arm on FSU linebacker Geno Hayes, who had bragged during the week that the Seminoles were going to knock Tebow out of the game.

Tebow did suffer a broken right hand when he was hit by another player as he crossed into the end zone, but he continued to play. He ran for another score and threw for three touchdowns as Florida won 45–12. Tebow had become the first player in Division I history to run for 20 scores and pass for 20 touchdowns, and that was good enough to beat out Arkansas running back Darren McFadden for the Heisman.

Tebow added to his totals in the Capital One Bowl and finished with 32 touchdown passes and 23 touchdown runs. The latter total was the fourth best in the nation. Tebow also threw only six interceptions during the season to finish with the SEC's top passing percentage at 66.9 percent. He totaled 3,286 passing yards and 895 rushing yards.

# 28 The Trailblazers

College football was slow to integrate—so slow that black players used to refer to their underground railroad, which took high school seniors up north to schools such as Michigan State to play the sport, even though integration had started in 1958. There was plenty of resistance in the South. Kentucky was the first school to sign African Americans when it gave scholarships to Nat Northington and Greg Page in 1966. At Florida it was even slower because counties in the state were fighting the Supreme Court's orders to integrate the student bodies.

Coach Ray Graves finally was able to bring in two African American players in 1968. On December 17 he signed running back Leonard George from Tampa, Florida. The next day he signed wide receiver Willie Jackson from Sarasota, Florida, by way of Valley Forge (Pennsylvania) Prep. "People advised me it was not a good choice," George said. "I was told I'd run into a lot of prejudice, and it wouldn't be a good situation."

The players had to endure racial slurs and taunts, especially when they faced road games at schools that had yet to integrate their football teams. "We wanted to show them we were just like anybody else and we had the ability to compete in the classroom," Jackson told *The Gainesville Sun* in 1991. "Back then we didn't look at ourselves as pioneers. We just wanted to play football and get an education."

George and Jackson played their first varsity games on September 12, 1970. Alabama and Georgia wouldn't have any black players for another year. LSU and Ole Miss didn't have any for two more years. Yet by 1973 Florida's roster was one-third African American.

It wasn't easy. In 1971 the Black Student Union at Florida staged a protest over the treatment black students were facing on campus. There were 66 arrests at the protest, and many students and faculty members left the school. Jackson spoke for the 10 athletes who would stay, saying they wanted to "give this thing a chance." Four of the athletes were baseball players, two were freshman basketball players, and four were track athletes.

Jackson had a solid career at Florida. He caught 75 passes for 1,170 yards and eight touchdowns. He also returned kicks and went on to play in the fledgling World Football League in Jacksonville, Florida. George became the first African American player to score a touchdown at Bryant-Denny Stadium, which he did on September 26, 1970 during a 46–15 loss in Tuscaloosa, Alabama. George was moved to defensive back after his sophomore season and became a two-year starter there.

They didn't consider themselves pioneers, but somebody had to get it started and put up with the negativity and controversy that would come with being first. This was a conference where the Confederate flag was waved proudly in the stands after big plays.

Unfortunately, in some places it still is.

# 29 Gatorade

It seemed like a simple question. Dwayne Douglas, a Florida assistant coach who had played for more than a decade in the NFL, approached Dr. Robert Cade, a kidney specialist at the University of Florida. Douglas had lost dozens of pounds in each game he played, but he never felt the need to go to the bathroom. He wanted to know why. Cade and three colleagues—Dana Shires, James Free, and Alejandro de Quesada—found that answer. The body lost so much water, salt, and electrolytes during exercise that there was never any reason to relieve yourself. But how could they replace that lost energy?

The year was 1965, and the great experiment was about to begin, one that would start an industry. Cade and his friends figured that if they could concoct a drink that would put salt and sugar—in addition to the water the players were used to drinking during football games—back into their systems perhaps it would give them an edge late in games when their opponents became weaker.

So he approached Florida coach Ray Graves with an idea. After coming up with a formula, Cade needed some guinea pigs. Graves didn't want to take any chances with his varsity team—which included quarterback Steve Spurrier—but he allowed Cade to experiment with 10 freshmen players. When those freshmen led a late comeback in a scrimmage against the B teamers, Graves asked for some of this new drink to be made available for the varsity's next game against fifth-ranked LSU. Not all the players were thrilled with the taste of the new drink—All-American tackle Larry Gagner spit it out and said the water tasted like urine—but Florida won the game 14–7, and Graves became a proponent.

The drink was called "Cade's Ade" or "Cade's Cola" until 1966 when Free came up with the name Gatorade. Cade's wife, Mary, suggested using a lemon-lime flavoring to help the taste, and after Florida beat Georgia Tech in the 1967 Orange Bowl, Stokely-Van Camp wanted to mass market the drink. Cade offered the rights to UF in exchange for money for marketing and manufacturing, but the school balked. Cade sold to Stokely, and Gatorade took off, eventually being marketed in 80 countries.

Stokely wanted a less regional name and experimented with several before deciding to retain Gatorade. Florida's rival schools tried to come up with their own drinks, so they wouldn't be caught drinking something with "Gator" as part of the name, but energy drinks like "Bulldog Punch" and "Seminole-ade" never caught on. Stokely came up with the formula for the taste you experience now when swigging a cold Gatorade. Ironically, when the Florida players first tasted the new Gatorade, they thought it was too sweet.

Cade tried to market some spin-offs of the product—most notably a beer called Hop 'N' Gator—but it never did much in the marketplace. After experimenting with the 25 percent alcohol beer, Cade was pulled over on his bike by a police officer who issued Cade a $15 ticket for riding too fast.

Although Cade passed away in 2007, the Cade Museum of Innovation and Invention is expected to break ground in Gainesville in 2015.

# 30 The 1997 FSU Game

By the time Florida reached its final regular season game of the 1997 season, Steve Spurrier had tried just about everything at

## Florida's Biggest Comeback

Although Florida has enjoyed plenty of come-from-behind wins, the biggest ever fourth-quarter comeback was from an 18-point deficit at Kentucky in 2003. It was freshman quarterback Chris Leak's first start, and the Gators could do little right on offense. It appeared that the Wildcats would end Florida's 16-game winning streak in the series.

But Florida caught a break when a Kentucky penalty on a UF punt kept a drive alive. The Gators then scored on a pass from Leak to Carlos Perez. Florida pulled closer when Leak hit Perez on a 10-yard touchdown pass on a fourth-down play.

On the next possession, Kentucky quarterback Jared Lorenzen dropped back to pass. Linebacker Channing Crowder was about to pounce on the husky quarterback, but Lorenzen stayed upright long enough to fling a pass into the arms of cornerback Johnny Lamar, who returned it 35 yards to the Kentucky 1-yard line. Ran Carthon scored two plays later to give Florida the 24–21 lead.

Kentucky's Taylor Begley would miss a 50-yard field goal with 44 seconds to play, and Florida escaped with another win against the hard-luck Wildcats.

quarterback. He started the year with sophomore Doug Johnson as his guy. Johnson led Florida to five straight wins and the No. 1 ranking in the country. But Florida lost its sixth game 28–21 to LSU, and the following Monday, Spurrier learned that Johnson had broken curfew the previous Thursday night.

Johnson was with several other players in downtown Gainesville that night. They were not suspended, but Johnson was. Spurrier always treated his quarterbacks a little differently. That meant freshman Jesse Palmer would get the start the following week at Auburn. Palmer struggled mightily, and the Gators turned to Noah Brindise, a senior who had rarely played. Brindise, a pudgy quarterback who transferred from Ursinus College, was given the nickname "Fat Dog" by his teammates.

Brindise led Florida to the win against Auburn with some help from wide receiver Jacquez Green, who became the first UF player to throw, catch, and run for a score in the same game. But a loss the next week to Georgia and some more musical chairs at quarterback left Florida at 8–2 heading into the Florida State game. The Seminoles were ranked No. 1 in the coaches poll and appeared headed to their second straight national title game.

But Spurrier came up with an innovative idea for the last game. He alternated Johnson and Brindise on every play, so there would be no questions about the play that had been called and he could "coach up" the quarterbacks between plays. "I wasn't a big fan of it," Johnson said. "I believed a quarterback should stay in the game to get a feel for things."

In one of the best games ever played at The Swamp, the Seminoles led 29–25 after a Sebastian Janikowski field goal. Janikowski incensed the crowd by performing the Gator Chomp after the kick. Florida took over at its 20 with 2:33 to play. On the sideline Spurrier came up with a new play he wanted to run and huddled the offense together. "We went on the field, and I asked the guys if they knew what we were going to run, and none of them did," Johnson said. "So I just called a protection and signaled to Jacquez to run a hitch-and-go because [defensive back] Samari Rolle was playing up on him."

Johnson threw a perfect pass to Green who was behind the defense. Green cut back across the field before being tackled at the FSU 18-yard line. "I was running on the sidelines with my hands on Coach Spurrier's shoulders, asking if he wanted me to go in," Brindise said, "but he wanted to leave Doug in at that point."

With Johnson still in at quarterback, Florida ran a draw play to Fred Taylor, who had lost two fumbles in the game, and he moved the ball to the 1-yard line. On the next play, Taylor punched it in for his third touchdown of the game and a 32–29 lead. Although

Gators fans were losing their minds over this sudden turn of events, they also worried that the three-play drive had been too quick. They remembered the 1994 game when the Seminoles scored 28 fourth-quarter points to tie UF.

But after FSU quarterback Thad Busby threw two incomplete passes, Gators linebacker Dwayne Thomas intercepted Busby's third effort. The linebacker laid flat on his back while his defensive teammates mobbed him, and Florida ran out the clock for the stunning win. Brindise took the final snaps, waving the ball in a windmill fashion after taking the final knee. "There was no way I wasn't going to be out there at the end," he said.

# 31 The Ring of Honor

If there was ever a special year for Florida football, it was 2006. Not only did Florida win a national championship that season, but the school also celebrated 100 years of college football in style. One of the biggest events was the creation of a Ring of Honor to commemorate the greatest players in Florida history. Well, some of them anyway.

The criteria was written in a way that made few players eligible, and four former players were initially inducted. To allow a fifth player, Wilber Marshall, to receive induction, an additional category was added the following year. Marshall attended—at a cost of $50,000 for his table—the lavish banquet the night before the first class would be honored in 2006. The next day Marshall found out he was left out of the Ring of Honor. According to *Florida Today* columnist Peter Kerasotis, an upset Marshall left the Alabama game the following day at halftime. "I guess I'm just sad," he told the columnist.

To Florida's credit, the University Athletic Association fixed the problem the following year, rewriting the criteria to include players with two or more consensus All-America honors, an impressive distinction that Marshall had accomplished. The criteria now reads as follows:

- Heisman Trophy winners
- Former UF All-Americans inducted into Pro Football Hall of Fame for accomplishments as players
- Former UF All-Americans who are NFL career category leaders
- Collegiate career category leaders
- Coaches with UF national championships
- Coaches with at least three UF SEC championships
- Players with two or more consensus All-American honors (AP, Walter Camp, *Sporting News*, AFCA, FWAA, UPI) who have also been named National Offensive/Defensive Players of Year (AP, Walter Camp, *Sporting News*, ABC, AFCA, FWAA, UPI)

Emmitt Smith, Steve Spurrier, Danny Wuerffel, and Jack Youngblood made up that first class. In 2007 Marshall was included. "I was disappointed [last year]," Marshall said during a conference call in 2007. "I didn't understand all that was going on. I understand now that there were some glitches. I'm glad it's being done now."

No one would question the five players who are in the Ring of Honor, but under its criteria great Gator players from the past such as Carlos Alvarez and Wes Chandler can never be voted in by the committee, which includes boosters, UAA officials, and former players. Those former stars don't meet the requirements. A player such as Lomas Brown, who may have been the best offensive lineman to ever play at Florida, has to hope that somehow he is elected to the Pro Football Hall of Fame.

However, on that beautiful day in Gainesville in 2006, nobody really cared about the criteria or who was left out. Three of the four inductees attended. Smith could not attend because he was training for *Dancing With the Stars*. The signs with the players' names were originally placed on the small wall in the north end zone that separates the Touchdown Terrace from the lower bowl but were moved to the top of the north end zone before Marshall's 2007 induction.

Two others have met the criteria, but each must wait five years before receiving induction. Urban Meyer qualifies in 2015 as a coach of two national championship teams, and Tim Tebow qualifies in 2014 as a Heisman Trophy winner. There's no question that Tebow, perhaps the most popular player in Florida history, will be voted in as soon as he is eligible. What to do about Meyer, whose popularity in the Gator Nation was crippled when he sat out a year before becoming the head coach at Ohio State, will be a more interesting decision.

# Spread the Ashes

While riding his mower to give the playing surface at The Swamp a trim, Bryce Rou has seen them. He knows what they're up to. And eventually when he reaches that part of the field, he will see the remains of a loyal Gators fan. "I have definitely seen some ashes," said Rou, who works for UF's turf management department. "You'll see someone kind of slowly walking on the field and you know what they're doing."

For some Florida fans, it is the ultimate resting place. The University Athletic Association doesn't encourage the spreading of ashes on its football field, but it's hardly a secret that it happens.

"We know that if we allowed weddings and funerals at the stadium, the requests would be endless," said Mike Hill, the executive associate athletic director for internal affairs. "We haven't had any weddings, but we've had some funerals."

Often it's as simple as taking the ashes in a bag and letting them trail behind as a grieving family member walks on the playing surface. Some ashes are spread throughout the stadium—some in the seat where the deceased had season tickets. It may sound ghoulish, but is it really that different than having your ashes spread at sea?

Fans also have made countless requests for marriage proposals either on the video board or at a certain part of the stadium. Those are not encouraged either, but more than one couple has made it down the 50-yard line late at night for the big moment. Some events, like charity functions, are permitted in the stadium, but those have to be managed. "Ever since we built the Touchdown Terrace and the Stadium Club, it has become like managing a hotel property," Hill said. "We have people who manage that, but we have to be restrictive because it has become a full-time job."

The Swamp, though, has become a memorable place for families who come in to get their pictures taken or just walk around one of college football's top venues because The Swamp is almost always open. "When I go around the country," said Chip Howard, executive athletic director for external affairs, "that's the thing that people can't believe. They are always asking me, 'You leave your stadium open?'"

It is only closed from late Thursday to two hours before a home game. That gives time for law enforcement to sweep the stadium, and for UF staff to prepare it for a game. The rest of the time, The Swamp could be referred to as a Gator Gym. It's rare that you walk into the stadium and not see someone running the stadium steps. That could include Becky Burleigh's soccer team, a physical education class, or Gainesville residents getting in a workout.

One of the most popular ways to break a sweat is to run the stadium bleachers row by row to the top—90 rows high. When you are out of breath—and even if your iron lungs are not—the view from the top can be dizzying. Doing "the Snake" is another popular exercise. You start at the bottom of the stadium, which is below ground level, and run the aisle to ground level. That's 32 steps (27 in the south end zone), and then you can go over to the next aisle, down and up, and so on. Some run the Touchdown Terrace ramp. The ramp that leads to the section in the north end zone is very steep, and the race up it can seem endless.

Whether you grieve, run, or walk, there are plenty of options for activity at The Swamp even when there is not a game.

# How the Gators Got Their Name

There are three versions of the story of how the Florida Gators became the Florida Gators. It would seem like an obvious nickname with all of the alligators in north central Florida. Heck, you don't even have to leave campus to see alligators. There's a reason why the university golf course discourages divers from going ball hunting in their ponds.

Let's look at the three possibilities:

1. Phillip Miller opened the first wholesale and retail grocery store in Gainesville, and it became a popular hangout for the college students. In 1907 Miller went to visit his son, Austin, who was in law school at the University of Virginia, and they visited the Michie Company. The company sold pennants and flags, and Phillip Miller thought it would be a good idea to get some of the fledgling football program. The team had no nickname, but Austin

Miller mentioned that there were a lot of alligators in Gainesville. So that became the image on the pennant, but only after Austin went to the library to find a picture of one for the manufacturer.

2. A player on the 1911 team named Neal Storter was given the nickname Bo Gator and eventually became the team's captain. He started the Bo Gator Club, a frivolous group of students who became more of a myth than a club. A former player named Roy Corbett sent a letter to *The Gainesville Sun* congratulating the 1928 team on its 8–1 season and mentioned that the nickname for the team had come from Storter's nickname.

3. Storter later denied the above claim and instead said the nickname "Gators" came from a reporter in Macon, Georgia, who

## Uniform Change

Like most major college football programs, the University of Florida has no choice at times. If Nike wants it this way, it will be that way. Add in the penchant of players who want to wear something different, and the team could end up wearing anything.

Back in the 1960s, the home uniform featured simple blue jerseys with white pants and a block "F" on the side of the helmet, though for the 1962 Gator Bowl, players pasted Confederate flags on the sides of their helmets.

When Doug Dickey took over, he introduced the interlocking U and F to the helmets. Charley Pell changed the color of Florida's home jerseys from blue to orange and also introduced the "Gators" script on the helmets. Steve Spurrier thought the orange jerseys looked too much like Clemson and went back to the blue. On the road under Spurrier, Florida would wear white jerseys with orange, blue, or white pants. Three times (all losses) Florida has worn blue tops with orange pants.

Nike put the Gators in throwback jerseys for the 2006 Alabama game with the block "F" on the helmets and in more modern Nike Pro Combat uniforms in 2009 and 2010. The Gators brought back the orange jerseys against LSU in 2010 and against Florida Atlantic the following year.

referred to a game that Florida was playing against Georgia in 1911 and wrote that the state was "being invaded by a bunch of alligators." It stuck and was later shortened.

The Miller version is the most commonly accepted version, and there seems to be a consensus that the colors orange and blue came from that meeting at the Michie Company. Because Virginia had those same colors, those choices were the most plentiful.

Decades later another major part of the UF tradition, which complements the Gators nickname, would be invented—The Chomp. Members of the Florida band in Jackson, Mississippi, for the Florida-Mississippi State game in 1981 started that distinct motion, which has become synonymous with the University of Florida.

# John J. Tigert

There are a handful of buildings on the University of Florida campus that every student spends some time in at some point of his or her college career. And if there is one building that Gainesville residents pass by almost daily, it's Tigert Hall. The administrative building has been the scene of crying fits over an unavailable class or a flat tire that made a student too late to drop/add one. But it's doubtful that many of these students have stopped to reflect on the building's namesake.

Although Florida has had plenty of prominent presidents through the years, John J. Tigert has been as influential to the Gators football program as any of them. Tigert had a resume in sports and public service when he was named UF's fourth president in 1928. He had played four sports—including football—at Vanderbilt and coached football and women's basketball at Kentucky. He earned a masters and a Rhodes scholarship, competing in cricket and rowing while in England. From 1921 to 1928, Tigert served as the United States commissioner of education. Then he came to UF.

The university, like the rest of the country, was going through some tough times financially, and Tigert could brilliantly stretch a dollar. By 1930 he was confident enough in his position to suggest that Florida needed its own football stadium. Until then the Gators had played in Fleming Field, which is now the north parking lot. Fleming Field also served as the baseball stadium for the school. Tigert, who never drew his full salary while at Florida, raised the $118,000 necessary to build the stadium and picked the site to the west of the swimming pool. All of the times you have walked up to the stadium, well, it's because that's where Tigert decided it should go.

Tigert was also a major factor in the formation of the Southeastern Conference. The presidents of the Southern Conference, to which Florida belonged, met in Knoxville, Tennessee, in 1933, and 13 of them split away to form the SEC. It was Tigert who had pushed for the move and then made the announcement. He served as the SEC president twice—from 1934 to 1936 and 1945 to 1947.

He wasn't finished.

Tigert was a big proponent of the scholarship, a grant-in-aid for student-athletes. At the 1946 NCAA Convention, Tigert and the SEC came under attack by other schools who didn't think players should receive money. But five years later, Tigert and the SEC found enough votes to win the battle on the convention floor, and that gave birth to the modern day scholarship. While also serving on the national rules committee, Tigert rewrote many of the regulations that are used in college football today.

In 1951 the university completed a building on the eastern edge of the campus, which Tigert had started during the final years of his presidency. The building would house the president's office and other administrators. In 1960 it was named Tigert Hall.

Tigert, whose accomplishments on campus can be seen every day, passed away in 1965 and was elected to the College Football Hall of Fame as well as the University of Florida Athletic Hall of Fame.

# Spurrier's Last Ride

The press conference had finished, and a reporter hounded Steve Spurrier as he left the Miami Beach hotel. Spurrier's Florida team had just clobbered Maryland 56–23 in the Orange Bowl, and he just wanted to get into his car with his wife, Jerri, and drive north to his condominium in Crescent Beach.

Crescent Beach has been a second home to Spurrier, a place to get away and have a few beers no matter where he has been coaching. A dinner at his favorite restaurant—Matanzas Inlet—would be waiting for the Spurriers that night, but first there was something that needed to be done. The man who had named The Swamp, who had brought the ultimate glory to the Gator Nation, and who had changed the culture of Florida football forever, had to resign.

He went to the condo owned by longtime friend and Florida sports information director Norm Carlson to pick up Carlson and his wife, Sylvia, for dinner. Spurrier told Carlson to get a beer; Jerri told Sylvia to get a glass of wine. They both needed to sit down. "I think he thought I was going to faint," Carlson said. Spurrier pulled out a three-page handwritten letter of resignation. "I thought he was kidding," Carlson said.

But then they went to work on it, refining it before its release the next day. In the letter Spurrier expressed his great appreciation for the opportunity Florida had given him and the support he had received while serving as UF's coach for 12 seasons. But he said he wanted to try the NFL.

"If that opportunity does not happen," he wrote, "I'll simply be a retired ball coach, rooting for the Gators in every sport."

Spurrier had flirted with the NFL before. In the spring of 1995, he nearly accepted a job with the Tampa Bay Buccaneers where he had finished his NFL career as a quarterback. He also had serious talks with New Orleans in 1997 and came close to taking that job. (Instead the Saints hired Mike Ditka.) He had talked to Washington and turned down the Redskins after the 2000 season because he knew he had a special team at Florida in 2001, but there were several reasons why Spurrier pulled the trigger in January of 2002.

1. "I simply believe that 12 years as head coach at a major university in the SEC is long enough," Spurrier wrote in his resignation letter. Spurrier was itching to try something else. As it turned out, he lasted only two seasons with the Redskins.

2. Expectations had grown out of whack. Florida had won 10 games in 2001, lost two games by a total of five points, and finished third in the final Associated Press poll, and it was considered a down year.

3. Spurrier was upset that his criticism of Florida State's Darnell Dockett, whom Spurrier accused of intentionally trying to hurt two of his players, fell on deaf ears with the UF administration the week before the Tennessee game.

Mostly, it was just time.

*After 12 years coaching Florida, Steve Spurrier threw his visor into the NFL ring where he guided the Washington Redskins from 2002 to 2003.*

## Florida's Winningest Coaches

| Name | Record | Years |
|------|--------|-------|
| Steve Spurrier | 122–27–1 | 1990 to 2001 |
| Ray Graves | 70–31–4 | 1960 to 1969 |
| Urban Meyer | 65–15 | 2005 to 2010 |
| Doug Dickey | 58–43–2 | 1970 to 1978 |
| Bob Woodruff | 53–42–6 | 1950 to 1959 |
| Galen Hall | 40–18–1 | 1984 to 1989 |
| Charley Pell | 33–26–3 | 1979 to 1984 |
| Charles Bachman | 27–18–3 | 1928 to 1932 |
| G.E. Pyle | 26–7–3 | 1909 to 1913 |
| Ron Zook | 23–14 | 2002 to 2004 |

After Spurrier and Carlson finished the letter, Spurrier called Florida athletic director Jeremy Foley. When he told Foley he was resigning, he was greeted by dead air. "Are you still there, Jeremy?" Spurrier said.

Foley was stunned. He had dealt with the possibilities before with Spurrier, but Foley felt like he had secured the coach with a $2.1 million a year contract. This one seemed to come out of nowhere. Spurrier then called his children to let them know. By morning the word had leaked out through an in-law of one of those children. *The Gainesville Sun* reported on its website that Spurrier was resigning. This was news to the Florida assistant coaches, who found out on the scrawl on ESPN while performing exit interviews with seniors.

Spurrier called his secretary Nancy Sain to let her know he was leaving. "We know, Coach. It's all over the place," she told him. Gator Nation was blown away. Two days later Spurrier held a press conference, his final one as the Florida coach.

# 36 The Gator Flop

A group of Florida football fans had piled into two SUVs and were heading to Columbia, South Carolina, for an SEC game when they stopped north of Jacksonville, Florida, at a gas station. As they piled out of the two cars, a man dressed in Miami colors from head to foot shouted at them, "You gonna flop in this game, too?"

The women retreated, and the men readied for a brawl as the Miami fan approached, then pivoted and returned to the car, screeching his tires, and shouting obscenities as he left. Some wounds never scab over.

Forget that this incident happened in 2007 and that the two teams had played each other three times in the previous 19 years. There has always been an underlying bitterness about this series, and a lot of it came to the forefront during the 1971 game. It should have been a nothing game. Miami came in at 4–5, and Florida was 3–7, a particularly disappointing season considering the 1969 Super Sophs were now seniors.

But the transition from Ray Graves to Doug Dickey as head coach after the 9–1–1 season in 1969 had left the remaining players angry and bitter. An All-American wide receiver, Carlos Alvarez, had tried to start an Athletes Union on campus to fight for the rights of players. Several players quit the team in Dickey's first year (1970), including All-SEC linebacker Fred Abbott, who later returned to the team. It was a mess that first year and did not get any better in 1971 as Dickey tried to move the offense from a pro-style passing attack to an option style. Watching quarterback John Reaves, a 6'4" drop-back gunslinger who would become a first-round NFL draft pick, try to run the offense was like watching your grandfather try to hook up a DVR.

## The Unbreakable Record

The record for total passing yards in a career set by John Reaves in 1971 didn't last long, It was broken seven years later by Washington State quarterback Jack Thompson, but one Reaves record is still going strong.

In a 1969 game against Auburn, Reaves threw nine interceptions in a game, an amount that is hard to fathom and unlikely to be broken.

Florida came into the game unbeaten and ranked seventh in the country but lost 38–12 as Auburn's zone defense gave Reaves fits. Even though Reaves was having an off day, it did not stop the Gators from throwing. He attempted 66 passes in the game, which is still the most passes attempted by a Florida quarterback. His 33 completions in the game are tied for the second most ever by a Gator.

By the time the Gators went to the Orange Bowl to finish their regular season, all of their hopes had been squashed like love bugs on a windshield. But there were reasons to play hard. It was their last game together, a lot of them were from Miami, and it was a big rivalry game. And if Reaves threw for 345 yards in the game, he would tie the all-time NCAA record for career passing yards. It wasn't like this was some long-standing, untouchable record. It had been set a year earlier by Stanford's Jim Plunkett. But it was something for which to strive.

Reaves was on fire that night in Miami, and the game was especially big for Alvarez, who had emigrated from Cuba to Miami as a young boy. In his first return to South Florida as a sophomore in '69, Alvarez caught 15 passes, which still stands as a UF single-game record.

On this night he again exploited the Miami defense, and Florida rolled over the Hurricanes. They led 38–8 late in the game when Reaves got the ball back for what he thought was one last chance at the record. By the latter part of the fourth quarter, everyone on the Florida sideline knew what was at stake—a consolation prize to a dreary season. Florida's defense held and forced a punt, but in an unappreciated move, team captain Harvin Clark returned the Miami punt 82 yards for a score with 7:44 to play in the game. After he scored, Clark sprinted to Reaves on the sideline and apologized. Miami got the ball back and started running its new wishbone formation to eat up yards and the remaining clock. Finally the Hurricanes were forced to punt, but Reaves forced a pass into the middle of the field, and it was intercepted. With the ball back, Miami had less interest in scoring than keeping the ball from Reaves.

Clark twice called timeout and begged Dickey to let Miami score, so Reaves could have one more shot at the record. Finally Dickey agreed, but the coach was stunned when he saw what transpired.

The Florida defenders didn't just let Miami score. As Miami quarterback John Hornibrook rolled to his left, most of the Gator defense flopped to the ground—bellies first. Clark went to his back because a neck injury made it difficult for him to lie on his front. One player did not flop—safety John Clifford from Coral Gables, located right near Miami's campus. "You look at the tape or any pictures, and I did not flop," he said. "It doesn't make what I did any more honorable, but I didn't flop."

After all that, Reaves almost threw an interception when Florida received the ball back, but on the second play of the drive, he hit Alvarez for 15 yards and the record. Miami coach Fran Curci was so incensed that he refused to shake Dickey's hand after the game.

The Florida players couldn't have cared less. They were so ecstatic to have a positive ending to a dreadful season that they stormed the field and into the pool at the Orange Bowl that housed Flipper, the dolphin mascot for the NFL's Miami Dolphins.

# 37 The Gator Walk

When Urban Meyer announced that he was starting this new tradition at Florida, the obvious question was—why didn't anyone think of that before?

Florida's football team previously bussed from the team hotel only a few miles away and ducked into the south end of the stadium down a ramp to the home locker room. "I used to love it," said linebacker James Bates, who played from 1993 to 1996. "I would start walking up and down the bus and getting everyone fired up, and there would always be fans of the opponents there waiting for us. They'd be yelling and banging on the bus. That got me fired up."

But Meyer wanted his players to be encouraged as they walked into the stadium and he changed the gameday culture at UF when he introduced the Gator Walk. It was hardly a novel idea as schools like Auburn and Tennessee already had their own versions. But it was something new at Florida in 2005.

The first Gator Walk took place before the opener that season against Wyoming, and the crowd was a little unsure of what to expect. "It was pretty cool," said offensive lineman Phil Trautwein. "That first Gator Walk was something that nobody had ever experienced before."

The buses stop on University Avenue, and the players are greeted by Gators fans who form a tunnel that leads to the bricked sidewalk into the north end of the stadium. Florida fans can purchase those bricks for $100 to $500. As they walk on the sidewalk that crosses Fleming Field—where Florida used to play before The Swamp was built—the fans on both sides cheer and reach to slap skin with their favorite players.

Florida fans used to time their arrival to the stadium based on how long they wanted to tailgate. But now they have to time it around the Gator Walk because traffic is backed up on University Avenue. You are either a fan who wants to be there in time, or one who wants to wait until it's over.

For the Gator Walk, Meyer had the team arrive with its police escort two hours before the game. Current Florida coach Will Muschamp likes to get to the stadium a little earlier, and the tradition takes place two hours and 15 minutes before kickoff. The players make their way through the crowd and past the Gators band into the stadium. They walk down the 32 flights of stairs, take a portable stairway to the field, and walk the length of the field to the locker room at the other end.

The Gator Walk usually goes off without incident, but before the 2008 game against LSU, Tim Tebow added some spice to it. It was a huge game for Florida, and Tebow wanted to make sure the crowd had its game face on. So as he walked through the Gator Walk, he began screaming, "Let's Go! Let's Go!" and gyrating with his arms.

# 38 Go Bowling

There aren't a lot of things the average fan can count on when it comes to their favorite college football team. When the season begins, no team is assured of a winning record, and no fan base can be guaranteed of postseason play. But Florida fans can certainly pencil a bowl game into their holiday planning. Florida has played in 22 straight bowls, the second longest active streak behind Florida State's 31.

During that streak it has not been a question of whether Florida will go bowling but where. Even in 2011 when the Gators went 6–6, they ended up in a New Year's Day bowl, defeating Urban Meyer's future team, Ohio State, in the Gator Bowl.

Florida's bowl history didn't begin until 1953 when the Gators were invited to the Gator Bowl. The Gator Bowl and the Sugar Bowl have been the most frequent homes for Florida, and UF has played in nine of each. But the Orange Bowl has been the friendliest for the Gators as UF has a 4–0 record in that game, including a win in the 2009 BCS National Championship Game.

Of Florida's 40 bowl games, a little more than half (22) have been played in the state of Florida. One of them was played in Gainesville. In 1973 Florida won its last five games to go 7–4, and the Gators were looking for a bowl game. But this was in the days when bowls lined up their teams long before the seasons ended, and the Gators looked like they might be left out. The Tangerine Bowl in Orlando had selected Miami (of Ohio) and East Carolina. But there were legal issues over the proposed expansion of the stadium in Orlando, and eventually East Carolina decided to withdraw from

## Bowl Records of UF Coaches

| | |
|---|---|
| Bob Woodruff | 1–1 |
| Ray Graves | 4–1 |
| Doug Dickey | 0–4 |
| Charley Pell | 2–2 |
| Galen Hall | 1–1 |
| Gary Darnell | 0–1 |
| Steve Spurrier | 6–5 |
| Ron Zook | 0–2 |
| Charlie Strong | 0–1 |
| Urban Meyer | 5–1 |
| Will Muschamp | 1–1 |

*(listed chronologically)*

the game. UF convinced the needy Tangerine Bowl that the game would need a bigger stadium than the 17,000-seater in Orlando, Florida. The Tangerine Bowl (now the Capital One Bowl) agreed, and Florida played a "home" bowl game against Miami of Ohio. The Redskins won 16–7 as the game was played in minus-4 degree temperatures, and Florida's players seemed like they just wanted to get off the field. Miami, by the way, was led by a defensive back named Ron Zook, who would later become the Florida coach.

Florida's success in bowl games has been up and down. The Gators are 20–20 in 40 bowl games, and much of the .500 record is because of Urban Meyer's stellar 5–1 mark in his six bowl games. There have been some amazing performances by Gators in bowl games and also by the opposition. Upset with his quarterback play, Steve Spurrier rode Fred Taylor, who ran for 234 yards on 43 carries, against Penn State in the 1998 Citrus Bowl. Tommie Frazier ran for 199 yards on 16 carries for Nebraska in the 1996 Fiesta Bowl. Frazier's 75-yard touchdown run was the signature play of the game as the quarterback shed Florida tacklers all the way down the field.

Tim Tebow went out with a bang as he threw for 482 yards in the 2010 Sugar Bowl, his final game as the Florida quarterback. He completed 88.6 percent of his passes, a BCS bowl game record. Michigan quarterback Chad Henne lit up a young Florida secondary in the 2008 Capital One Bowl. He completed 25-of-39 passes for 373 yards, the most a Florida team has allowed in a bowl game. After being injured for much of the 1999 season, Travis Taylor exploded in his final game as a Gator in the 2000 Citrus Bowl. He caught 11 passes for 156 yards and three touchdowns in the game. In that same game, Michigan State countered with Plaxico Burress, a one-time Florida commit. Burress caught 13 passes for 185 yards and three scores in leading Michigan State to the win.

# 39 Urban Meyer's Leave of Absence

Urban Meyer sat up in his bed like he was sprung from a catapult. He then collapsed to the bedroom floor while his wife, Shelley, called 911. So began a scary time for the Meyer family and one of the most bizarre periods in Florida football history.

It was the night after Florida had lost to Alabama in the SEC Championship Game 32–13 to spoil a perfect season and a shot at three national titles in four years. Meyer had been so consumed with chasing perfection he had forgotten how to live. He quit exercising and quit eating. During the previous summer, he had talked about how he had come to love the Gainesville community, including his lake house and church, and felt like he was at home. But once the season started, the grind was all that mattered.

He went from 217 pounds to 180. Food? There was no time for eating when there was video to break down. His family might as well have been someone else's. "I remember my first year at Florida. The night before my first Tennessee game, I went to see my son, Nate, pitch," he said. "I threw all that out the window."

Meyer was so obsessed with winning that a loss nearly killed him. Diagnosed with exhaustion and dehydration, he saw specialists around the country to find out what was wrong with him. They basically told him he had to back off his work schedule. So Meyer resigned. He met with Florida athletic director Jeremy Foley and president Bernie Machen for days as they tried to convince him to stay. But burned to a crisp, Meyer worried desperately about his health. "I was very concerned with where I was at," he said.

The announcement was made the day before Florida left for the Sugar Bowl. The team practiced the next morning before flying to New Orleans. "It was a cold day. This team had just had the rug pulled out underneath them," Meyer said. "They'd lost a chance to play for the national championship and now they had lost their coaches. And they were having their best practice of the year. [Strength and conditioning coach] Mickey Marotti got a hold of me about halfway through practice and started talking about all the people that my decision was going to impact. I couldn't just hand this job to somebody and let them start firing people."

So he called Foley from the practice field and asked for a meeting. In Foley's office Meyer lobbied for offensive line coach Steve Addazio to be named the new head coach. Foley said he had a lot of respect for Addazio, but he couldn't make that move. Instead he told Meyer he would make Addazio interim head coach. "Go take some time," Foley said. "See if you want to come back."

Meyer went to his office to think about it. He decided to give it a shot and announced that he would come back after taking some time off. Florida beat Cincinnati in the Sugar Bowl 51–24, and Meyer looked lost on the podium after the game. "I was thinking, *Did all this just happen?*" he said.

Addazio did the dirty work during the offseason while Meyer spent time overseas, took his son to Cooperstown, New York, and relaxed at his lake house in Melrose. As time went by, he felt healthier and gained his weight back. He started running again and spending more time with his family. And eventually Meyer declared himself ready to return to work. But the 2010 season was a difficult and rare one for the coach. Florida had lost not only talent to the NFL but also defensive coordinator Charlie Strong to Louisville. Despite struggling through home losses to LSU and Mississippi State, the Gators still found themselves in position to win the SEC East with a victory against South Carolina.

Instead the Gamecocks humbled the Gators 36–14. A 31–7 loss to Florida State finished the regular season. Meyer vowed to rebuild the program "the right way." But just 10 days after the game, he resigned again. "That season we didn't have a great team, but we fought," he said. "It didn't feel the same. It was all new, but the bottom line was that I couldn't get over the fact that I was killing myself. It just didn't feel right."

Meyer took a year off before taking the Ohio State job in December of 2011, claiming he finally had figured out how to balance his work, family, and life.

# 40 The Florida-Tennessee Rivalry

Considered one of the biggest rivalries in college football, the Florida-Tennessee matchup was a must-see game every time the two teams faced off. And it is still a big enough game that ESPN's *GameDay* came for the 2012 contest. But before the SEC expanded to 12 teams and shoved Florida and Tennessee into a corner, it wasn't much of a rivalry at all.

The two teams played only 21 times prior to 1992, and despite some memorable games, it was hardly considered a rivalry. In fact most of the bad blood between the two schools came from an off-the-field incident. Following the 1984 season, Tennessee led the charge to strip Florida of its first SEC title because of the Gators' NCAA probation. But Florida also took Doug Dickey away from Tennessee to become the UF head coach, and an urban legend exists that Tennessee watered the field before the 1928 game to slow down Florida's quick running backs.

The rivalry really started to crank up the year before expansion when Florida played host to Tennessee in a game between two top 10 teams. Thanks in part to Larry Kennedy's interception return

## Peyton's Follies

Peyton Manning had an amazing career at Tennessee. If not for Florida, it would have been even more special.

Manning was part of four straight losing efforts for the Vols against the Gators. He played briefly as a freshman in 1994 when Florida shut out Tennessee 31–0. In fact the Vols' poor offensive performance in that game helped pushed Manning into the starting lineup.

In 1995 Manning saw a 30–14 lead late in the second quarter turn into a blowout loss. In 1996 Florida scored the first 35 points of the game and won 35–29. With Danny Wuerffel no longer around in 1997, it seemed as if Manning finally would beat the Gators. But Tennessee couldn't cover Jacquez Green, and Florida got an interception return for a score from Tony George to win 33–20 in a battle of top five teams.

Losing to the mighty Gators may have cost Manning the Heisman Trophy that year. Some voters found it difficult to select a guy who had never beaten Florida. One consolation—Manning and the Vols finally won the SEC title that year when Florida faltered. And it wasn't a total loss for the Manning family. Peyton's brother, Eli, went 2–0 against the Gators from 2002 to 2003.

for a score, No. 10 Florida beat No. 4 Tennessee 35–18 on its way to the SEC title. Over the next 11 seasons, at least one of the two teams would be ranked in the top 10, and eight times both were top 10 teams. Steve Spurrier lost two of his first three games to the Vols before going on a run made that much more impressive by Tennessee's stature. When they played the Gators from 1993 to 1997, the Vols' average national ranking was 6.8, and yet Florida pulled off five wins in a row.

They did it with defense, beating the Vols 31–0 in Knoxville in 1994 and with offense, scoring 41 second-half points to come from behind to win 62–37 in 1995. The following year saw the most hyped Florida-Tennessee game yet as the Gators were ranked fourth, and the Vols were ranked second. Both teams had Heisman

Trophy candidates, and despite the game being only the third of the year, it was basically for the SEC East crown.

In the rain in Knoxville, Tennessee, Florida went for a fourth-and-11 on the first drive, and Danny Wuerffel hit Reidel Anthony for a touchdown pass on the play. That started a barrage of points that ended with Anthone Lott's scoop and score of a fumble to make it 35–0 barely into the second half. Florida ended up winning 35–29 as the game ended with a Tennessee onside kick recovered by Florida. "I don't know where all of those Tennessee fans went," linebacker James Bates said after the game. "Maybe *The Jeff Foxworthy Show* was on."

Tennessee pulled out a 20–17 overtime win in 1998 on its way to the national championship. Vols fans were so thrilled to finally beat Florida that students stormed the field and tore down an end-zone fence. The heat continued in 2000 when Jabar Gaffney caught the winning touchdown pass in Knoxville…for a second anyway. Gaffney caught the pass from Jesse Palmer and dropped it almost immediately, but it was ruled a catch, leading to Florida's win. With the game moved to the end of the 2001 season because of the 9/11 terrorist attacks on New York City, the Vols stunned Florida 34–32 in Gainesville. It turned out to be Steve Spurrier's last game in The Swamp as Florida's coach.

The rivalry continued its intensity during the Ron Zook years in part because he had been an assistant at Tennessee. And then it flamed brightly during the 2009 season when Tennessee coach Lane Kiffin publicly accused Urban Meyer of illegal recruiting tactics, which turned out to be perfectly legal. How badly did Florida want to get back at Kiffin? After a 10-point win, Florida players, coaches, and fans were disappointed in the margin. Derek Dooley had no luck against the Gators, and the rivalry has flickered a bit because the Vols haven't been ranked for this game since 2007. But Florida-Tennessee is still considered a major rivalry game.

# 41 The Kick

In 1966 Bob Griese had an incredible year for the Purdue Boilermakers. He threw for 1,888 yards, ran for six touchdowns, and led his team to its first Rose Bowl appearance. But he didn't have "the kick." As a result Griese finished second in that year's Heisman Trophy voting to Florida quarterback Steve Spurrier.

On October 29, 1966, unbeaten Florida faced Auburn on homecoming. It was a wild game that included an 89-yard kickoff return and a 93-yard fumble return for Tigers touchdowns. As a result the game was tied at 27 when Spurrier drove the Gators down the field to try to win it. "They couldn't stop us," Spurrier said.

When officials called Spurrier for intentional grounding to back Florida up to its own 30-yard line, it looked like the game would end in a tie. But he hit tight end Jack Coons for a seven-yard gain on third down. It would take a 40-yard field goal to win it.

"Wayne Barfield was a great short-range kicker," said Florida historian Norm Carlson, who was Florida's sports information director at the time. "But he could not have made that field goal." The other option, Spurrier, had tried three field goals during the season. He made two in a 43–7 win against Northwestern in the season opener and missed one later in the year against North Carolina State. He had the trainers keep a square-toed shoe in his equipment bag for field goal attempts. Florida called timeout, and Spurrier went to the sideline. He urged coach Ray Graves, "Let me kick it."

"It's funny, but it reminds me of my first year at South Carolina [as head coach in 2005]," Spurrier said. "We were down to Tennessee 15–13, and it was fourth-and-4. It would be a 48-yard field goal, and I was trying to decide what to do. And our kicker Josh Brown came up behind me and said, 'Field goal?' And he had that look in his eyes. So I said, 'Field goal. Let's go kick it.' And he made it, and we won the game. It was the same kind of thing."

Auburn hardly rushed the 40-yard attempt. Auburn coach Shug Jordan later told Carlson that one of his assistant coaches was adamant on the sideline it would be a fake. "Jordan told me that he said to a coach, 'I hope it is—because if he kicks it, he'll make it,'" Carlson said. "He loved Spurrier."

Holder Larry Rentz took the snap and accidentally spun the ball the wrong way so that the laces faced the kicker instead of the target. No worries. Spurrier drilled the kick through the uprights barely over the crossbar. "I hit it dead straight," Spurrier said. "But it didn't have a lot on it."

Spurrier said he grabbed the game ball once it was over and still has it in his house. He also has a Heisman Trophy, thanks largely to the kick. "It was typical Spurrier," Carlson said. "There were a bunch of national writers there. The Heisman ballots had to be in the next week. The timing couldn't have been better. It was the ideal moment for him. He has no nerves.

"It won him the Heisman, no question about it."

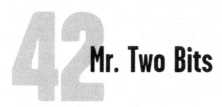

# Mr. Two Bits

So when was your first time? Probably you were sitting in the stands at Florida Field, and there was a lull in the action, and you first heard the whistle. You wondered why someone would bring a whistle to a football game. It could cause a disruption in play. That guy is going to get kicked out. That was your first time. By your second time, someone had explained it to you. And by your third time, you were hoping your section was next.

Mr. Two Bits was on the loose.

When George Edmondson, a fighter pilot in the Navy, returned to his hometown of Tampa, Florida, a friend asked him to a game. Florida was playing host to The Citadel, Edmondson's alma mater, to open the 1949 season. They settled into their seats at Florida Field, and when the Florida team came running onto the field, there were boos emanating from the crowd. "How do you boo your own team?" Edmondson later recalled that he asked his friend.

Gators fans were very disgruntled with the direction of the program. They went winless in 1946. They managed four wins in '47 but lost five of their last six games in '48. There was no reason to think it would be any better in '49 with Raymond "Bear" Wolf as the coach. On September 24 the crowd let them know it. Edmondson stood up in his seat and began an old high school chant that he remembered.

Two bits!
Four bits!
Six bits!
A dollar!
All for the Gators, stand up and holler!

A few people in his section stood. As the game went on, more people joined it. A legend was born.

Edmondson would return to Florida games with a bugle and a sign that read "2 BITS" while making his way around the stadium. As time went on, the bugle gave way to a more efficient whistle, and his uniform became standard—yellow shirt, light blue slacks, and orange-and-blue tie.

It would usually be early in the game when you would hear the whistle. Hey, he's in the north end zone. Look, he's over by the students. It was never intrusive and always classy. Named an honorary alumnus and selected to the Athletic Hall of Fame, Edmondson became a part of gameday tradition at Florida. He started a fund to help cheerleaders and has a golf tournament in Gainesville every year. The lounge at the campus' Hilton hotel is named for him.

Mr. Two Bits became so popular that Tampa Bay owner Hugh Culverhouse offered to pay Edmondson to bring the character to the Buccaneers' NFL games. Edmondson declined. His role was a labor of love, and Florida had become his adopted team.

After the 1998 season, Edmondson announced that failing health and age (he was 76 at the time) would force him to step away from his duties. He was given a game ball after the final home game that season and carried off the field on the shoulders of Florida's players. But Florida kept bringing him back for on-the-field performances before big games. He would blow the whistle, hold the sign to announce his presence, and then quiet the crowd before starting the cheer.

His last appearance came 10 years later when the Gators faced The Citadel. He then took his whistle home to Tampa.

Imitators have followed. Florida's mascot, Albert, often dons a yellow shirt and gets the crowd going with the cheer. During some games there will be a whistle in the stands and a feeble attempt to recreate the magic. But there was only one Mr. Two Bits.

# 43 Charlie Strong

If you want to trace the success of Florida football, have lunch with Charlie Strong. Nobody has a better feel for where Florida went from the mid-1980s to today better than the current head coach at Louisville.

Unfortunately for Florida the training he received as a Gators assistant backfired in the 2013 Sugar Bowl when his Louisville team beat Florida 33–23. Louisville wasn't supposed to have a chance, but one of Strong's strengths as a Gators assistant was his ability to motivate. He convinced players to play their best in the biggest games. "The University of Florida has a lot to do with any successes I have had," Strong said. "I loved it there."

His wild ride with the Gators began right out of college (Central Arkansas) when he landed a job as a graduate assistant under Charley Pell in 1983. Pell was fired three games into the next season, so Strong's second boss was interim coach Galen Hall. When Hall became the full-time coach, he hired Strong again in 1988 to coach linebackers. After Hall was fired, Strong left, but Steve Spurrier brought him back as an assistant head coach from 1991 to 1994. After stints at Notre Dame and South Carolina, Strong returned to Florida in 2002 to be Ron Zook's defensive coordinator.

When Zook was fired, Strong figured he was leaving as well. "I had been offered the defensive coordinator's job at Notre Dame by Charlie Weis," Strong said. "I was going to go. Urban Meyer and I talked, and he wanted me to stay. He was bringing in Greg Mattison and he wanted us to be co-coordinators. I remember the week of our bowl game when I was the interim head coach, and all the players were asking me if I was going to stay. The thing is I had a previous great relationship with Mattison and I knew we would work together. We were already in Gainesville, so why not stay?"

Meyer wanted Strong to bring discipline to a program lacking it. "You do that," Meyer told Strong, "and we'll win a national championship." Instead they won two.

After a try for a third one in 2009, Strong finally was offered a head coaching job. He had been turned down for so many

## From Assistants to Glory

A lot of great assistant coaches have come through Gainesville on their way to bigger and better jobs. Former players such as Chan Gailey and Mike Mularkey went on to become head coaches in the NFL. Here's a top 10 of UF assistants who went on to greatness.

1. **Steve Spurrier** (1978)—He enjoyed head coaching success at Florida and South Carolina.
2. **Frank Broyles** (1950)—He went on to become a great coach and athletic director at Arkansas.
3. **Mike Shanahan** (1980 to 1983)—The current Washington Redskins head coach won two Super Bowls as Denver Broncos head coach.
4. **Bob Stoops** (1996 to 1998)—He won a national title at Oklahoma and reinvigorated the program.
5. **Lindy Infante** (1968 to 1971)—He had several successful stints as an NFL head coach and also coached the USFL's Jacksonville Bulls.
6. **Pepper Rodgers** (1960 to 1964)—He won 73 games at three different schools.
7. **Tonto Coleman** (1950 to 1951)—He served as SEC commissioner from 1966 to 1972.
8. **Ken Hatfield** (1971 to 1977)—He had an excellent career as a head coach at Arkansas and Air Force.
9. **Dan Mullen** (2005 to 2008)—He has made Mississippi State relevant as the school's head coach.
10. **Bobby Pruett** (1994 to 1995)—He won an NCAA Division I-AA national championship at Marshall.

opportunities that he couldn't help but wonder about the race card. But Louisville changed all that. And he repaid the school after the 2012 season by turning down several schools (including Tennessee) who wanted to hire him.

He's no longer a Gator, but his career represents an amazing time line. How many people can say they worked for Pell, Hall, Spurrier, Zook, and Meyer?

# 44 Shane Matthews

During the 1990 spring football game, the Florida football team would be divided up into two squads—the orange and the blue—as usual. But this time there was a twist. Steve Spurrier put an assistant coach in charge of each team and held a draft. John Reaves, the quarterbacks coach and a former Florida star quarterback himself, had the first pick. He didn't take the incumbent quarterback Kyle Morris. Instead he picked Shane Matthews. "I was a little shocked when he picked me," Matthews said. "But he always thought I had a chance to be a good quarterback."

The spring game in Spurrier's first season was played in Jacksonville, Florida, at the Gator Bowl because Florida Field was being expanded. Matthews had a great spring game; Morris did not. "I felt bad for Kyle because he was a good friend," Matthews said. "And he still is today."

That spring game was the clincher for Spurrier, who was looking for a quarterback who could run his offense the way he envisioned it. He didn't need a powerful arm, but he had to have accuracy and a great understanding of the offense. "Being a coach's son, I understood what a coach wanted," Matthews said. "And Coach Spurrier and I thought the same way."

Matthews started that 1990 season and led Florida to a nine-win season. A year later, he led Florida to its first official SEC title. And as a senior behind a shaky offensive line, he guided Florida to the first ever SEC Championship Game. As a sophomore and junior, he was named the SEC Player of the Year. It was quite a comeback story for a guy who was well down the depth chart when Spurrier arrived.

Matthews was a star quarterback in Pascagoula, Mississippi, where his dad, Bill, coached the high school team. Tall and slender, Matthews was tougher than he looked and had the ability to find open receivers and precisely deliver a catchable ball. "If you're accurate, you're going to play," Matthews said.

He was heavily recruited and narrowed his choices to Florida, Florida State, Texas A&M, Ole Miss, and LSU. Because he wanted to play in the SEC, it ended up being a Florida-LSU recruiting battle. Florida's academics won out. "Really, if I'd never played a down, my parents would have been okay with it," Matthews said, "because they wanted me to get my degree."

His early years at Florida were frustrating. The Gators were a run-first team, and Matthews wasn't playing. Midway through the 1989 season, Matthews and three other players—including Morris—were suspended because a teammate had gone to the UF administration and told them the players were laying bets on games with a bookie in Athens, Georgia. They weren't betting on Florida's games, but the school, still reeling from NCAA sanctions and the dismissal of coach Galen Hall, was obviously concerned. "A lot of kids go through a lot of things," Matthews said. "It was hard. But we had a rule in my family that once you start something you're going to finish it."

Florida hired Spurrier and announced his return on New Year's Eve of 1989. By the time the Gators played Oklahoma State in the 1990 opener, Matthews was the man. And Matthews and the Spurrier offense not only took the SEC by storm, but also changed the league. Suddenly it wasn't enough to just run the ball and play defense. You had better be able to—as Spurrier would say—"pitch it around the ballfield."

Matthews finished his career with 74 touchdowns—fifth best all time at Florida. His 9,287 passing yards is the third most in school history. Only Chris Leak completed more passes as a

*Quarterback Shane Matthews, who threw for 9,287 yards and 74 touchdowns in his Florida career, barks out the play call during a 1992 victory against Kentucky.*

Gators player. "I don't think people realized how good we were," Matthews said. "That 1991 team was a really good team. We didn't have a whole lot of star guys, but we laid the foundation for what would come with Florida football."

Matthews went on to have a long NFL career with several teams, including the Redskins when Spurrier coached Washington. He started 22 NFL games during his 14 years in the league and finished in 2006 with 4,756 passing yards for his career. He is now the head coach at Nease High in St. Augustine, Florida.

# 45 Napolatano's—The Coaches' Favorite Postgame Place

Well after closing time at his restaurant, Dean Nappy didn't bother leaving—especially if the Gators had won a big road game. He had received the call several times, waking him from a deep sleep. "Deano, can you open the place up for us?" The voice on the other end of the phone was always Jamie Speronis, the director of football operations for Steve Spurrier. "This was before cell phones," Nappy said, "but they'd always find a phone just before they took off."

Nappy and his wife, Ginger, own Napolatano's, an Italian restaurant off Newberry Road in west Gainesville. Their son, Eric, was a placekicker on the team under Urban Meyer. (A framed No. 14 jersey of Eric Nappy, signed by the coaches, hangs on one wall at the restaurant.)

Because the restaurant is only a mile away from the affluent Haile Plantation area where all of the football coaches have lived over the last two decades, it's a frequent stop for the coaches. Will Muschamp often orders takeout from Napolatano's especially on

Wednesday nights because the special is mussels, a Muschamp favorite. The restaurant was also a favorite of Tim Tebow's, and there are several pictures of him on the walls. The restaurant also serves as a place where the coaches take recruits for dinner. "I remember when they were recruiting Jesse Palmer, and he had just watched them beat Auburn," Nappy said. "He came in here after the game, and the place was hopping and he said, 'I'm coming to Florida.'"

The tradition of hitting Napolatano's after a big road win started for Spurrier and the assistant coaches in 1994 after a 31–0 win against Tennessee. In 1994 Nappy built a secluded dining room in the back, so that Spurrier could have a place to eat without being overwhelmed by fans. Sometimes he'd enter through the back and walk through the kitchen. As they spooned marinara sauce over pasta, the kitchen workers had grown accustomed to seeing coaches in there. After a big win against Florida State when his defense had played well, then-defensive coordinator Ron Zook went into the kitchen, raised his arms, and yelled, "How 'bout them Gators!"

On a December night in 1994, Florida had won the SEC Championship in Atlanta, beating unbeaten and No. 3-ranked Alabama 24–23. Nappy knew not to go home after the restaurant closed at 11 PM. "Deano, can you stay up late!" The call came, and Nappy was ready with appetizers and cold beers. The coaches partied deep into the night. "I had to go to the kitchen and I came back out, and they were gone," he said. "They had all just split. There were empty bottles and chicken bones all over the table."

And one more thing—the SEC Championship Trophy. They had forgotten it.

Nappy put the trophy in his office, and the next day, his employees were blown away. They lined up to get their pictures taken with it. And finally, Speronis called. "Deano, have you seen the trophy?"

"What trophy?" Nappy joked.

Eventually the trophy was returned, but the late-night parties continued. There are classic pictures on the walls at Napolatano's of the coaches, including one of Bob Stoops, the Florida defensive coordinator before becoming Oklahoma's head coach, tending bar late at night with a cigar in his mouth after the Gators won the national championship.

Those pictures survived the fire that destroyed the original building in 2008. The Nappys built a new restaurant on the site, including a back dining room for special occasions—like after Florida takes home an SEC Championship Trophy.

# 46 The Bull Gator

He came to Gainesville from Georgia Tech and took a pay cut to do so. Nicknamed "the Bull Gator," Ray Graves brought his square jaw and monster defense to a place in desperate need of a consistent winner. Although he never quite got Florida over the top in the SEC, he certainly changed Florida football.

Graves won 70 games in 10 seasons as Florida's head coach. Until Steve Spurrier passed that total, Graves had the most wins in UF history. He also recruited some of the school's most legendary players, including Spurrier, Jack Youngblood, Larry Smith, and Carlos Alvarez. "Coach Graves was more than a coach," said Alvarez, a wide receiver on Graves' last team. "He was like a father to all of the players."

Graves played football in his hometown of Knoxville and was captain of the 1941 Tennessee Volunteers. He served as an unpaid Tennessee assistant before resigning in 1945 so that he could play for the NFL's Philadelphia Eagles. During his playing career, Graves tried to enlist in the Navy, but he was deaf in one ear and was turned away. He went full bore into coaching and helped lead Georgia Tech to prominence in the 1950s. The Yellow Jackets won the national title in 1952.

Graves started the monster defense, a new scheme that had a free safety and a strong safety in the defensive backfield. His success caught the attention of Florida administrators who had given coach Bob Woodruff 10 years to put the Gators on the national map and had seen only one season of more than six wins. They hired Graves, and he did not disappoint. In his third game as the Florida coach, his Gators stunned 10th-ranked Georgia Tech. Florida would win nine games for the first time in school history after beating Baylor in the Gator Bowl.

Graves' second year, when the Gators went 4–5–1, was his only losing record. A year later Florida surprised ninth-ranked Penn State 17–7 in the Gator Bowl, and in 1963 the Gators went to Tuscaloosa to hand Bear Bryant his first loss at Denny Stadium. In 1964 Graves unveiled a two-quarterback system with lefty Tommy Shannon and sophomore Spurrier. The latter led Florida to its first Sugar Bowl the following year and won the Heisman in 1966.

That Florida team won nine games by beating eighth-ranked Georgia Tech in the Orange Bowl. Florida football was at its highest peak, but it couldn't break through the ceiling. The Gators could never win an SEC title under Graves despite going 6–3–1 against Georgia. During Graves' tenure, the battle cry—"Wait 'Til Next Year"—was established. And it appeared that in 1968, next year *was* here.

With Smith at tailback, a veteran line led by All-American Guy Dennis, and a salty defense that included cornerback Steve Tannen, the Gators won their first four games and were ranked seventh in the nation by the Associated Press. But a hamstring injury hindered Smith, and Florida wasn't able to lean on the running game as

## Coaches of the Year

Ray Graves was presented with the SEC Coach of the Year Award as voted by the other SEC coaches in 1960. Here are the other UF coaches who have been honored by the coaches, the Associated Press, or United Press International.

1980—**Charley Pell** He took a winless team to eight wins in his second year.

1984—**Galen Hall** He took over as interim coach three games into the season and did not lose.

1990—**Steve Spurrier** In his first year, Spurrier led Florida to the best record in the SEC.

1991—**Steve Spurrier** Florida won its first official SEC crown.

1995—**Steve Spurrier** Gators had a perfect regular season and won SEC title game.

1996—**Steve Spurrier** He led Gators to their first national championship.

2012—**Will Muschamp** He shared the award with Texas A&M's Kevin Sumlin.

Despite winning two national titles and two SEC championships, Urban Meyer was never Coach of the Year in the conference but was the All-American Football Foundation's National Coach of the Year in 2006.

much as it would have liked. In Chapel Hill, North Carolina, it all came tumbling down. On a rainy day, Florida lost seven fumbles and the game 22–7. A week later the Gators tied Vanderbilt. Then they lost to Auburn on homecoming.

Graves had an idea to save the season. With quarterback coach Fred Pancoast in the hospital after an appendicitis attack, Graves switched coordinators. Defensive coordinator Gene Ellenson would coach the offense, and offensive coordinator Ed Kensler would coach the defense. There's a reason why more teams don't adopt this bizarre strategy. It looked like the offensive coach was coaching the defense and vice versa. In a rain that never let up, ninth-ranked Georgia won 51–0.

Even though Florida closed with two straight wins, Graves' crazy decision could not be ignored. The UF administration made him a deal—coach one more year and then stay on as athletic director. Graves agreed, and UF began working on luring Doug Dickey to Florida. But Graves' final season turned out to be one of the best ever at Florida. With sophomores John Reaves and Carlos Alvarez lighting it up, the Gators went 9–1–1 and won the Gator Bowl. But the decision to replace Graves had been made—much to the chagrin of the Florida players. "The thing about Coach Graves was that he took a special interest in his players and their life after their careers were done," Dennis said. "He wanted to make sure you were going to be a success in life. He was really a special man." As an example of that, 93 percent of his UF players graduated.

As athletic director, Graves helped usher in the rise of women's sports at Florida. He retired in 1979. When Spurrier passed his old coach for the most wins at UF, he brought Graves to the locker room and presented him with a game ball.

# 47 Florida's First Bowl Game

When Florida fans scan the rich football history of the Gators, it may surprise them to find out the team never played in a bowl game prior to 1953. (The 1912 squad played in a bowl game in Cuba that was not officially sanctioned as a bowl game.) When the Gators played in the Gator Bowl on January 1, 1953, there were only seven bowl games—a far cry from the 35 that are available now. It was a different time. There were not only fewer bowls, but also fewer Florida teams worthy of one.

## The Gainesville Gator Bowl

With a 90,000-seat stadium, you might wonder why Gainesville doesn't have its own bowl game.

Well, it did.

In 1994 the Gator Bowl was shut down while it was being renovated for the expansion Jacksonville Jaguars of the NFL. So the Gator Bowl was played in "The Swamp" that season. On December 30, 1994, a crowd of 62,200 saw Tennessee and Virginia Tech play in the game. All of the activities and interviews leading up to the game were held in Jacksonville, and the two teams bussed over on gameday.

Why didn't Florida play in the Gator Bowl in Gainesville? The Gators were in New Orleans to face Florida State in the Sugar Bowl.

Led by a freshman quarterback named Peyton Manning, the Volunteers jumped out to a 35–10 halftime lead and cruised to a 45–23 win. It was the only game Manning won in The Swamp, losing to Florida in the stadium in both 1995 and 1997. His brother, Eli, would fare better, beating UF 20–17 in 2003.

Florida football had been woeful in the 1940s under Thomas Lieb and Raymond "Bear" Wolf. They did not finish with a winning record in any of those years and went 0–9 in 1946. In 1950 Florida hired Bob Woodruff, and he was able to turn things around. Woodruff founded Gator Boosters and started raising the money necessary to get the program on track. His first teams both went 5–5, but his 1952 team won seven games in the regular season with stars such as Rick Casares, Doug Dickey, and Charlie LaPradd. LaPradd, a two-way player, became only the third All-American in UF history. The Gators suffered a tough 17–14 loss to third-ranked Georgia Tech in the second game of the season but bounced back to pound Georgia 30–0 and beat Auburn 31–21.

Florida would play in the appropriately named Gator Bowl. That bowl was started in 1946 by four Jacksonville, Florida, businessmen, who put up $10,000 to underwrite the game. It usually featured a team from the Southern Conference, but in 1953 it changed its affiliation to the Southeastern Conference. After expanding to seat 16,000 in 1948, the stadium changed its name from Fairfield Stadium to the Gator Bowl. By 1953 the capacity was 36,000, and an estimated crowd of 30,000 watched the Gators play in their first bowl game.

At 7–3 UF was ranked 15th in the nation when they faced a 12th-ranked, 8–1–1 Tulsa team. Tulsa was an eight-point favorite, but Florida came out with a brand new offense for the game, employing the belly option play. The Gators jumped out to a 14–0 lead using it. Casares scored the first touchdown on a 2-yard run, and Fred Robinson hit J. "Papa" Hall for a 37-yard touchdown pass. Casares made both extra points; the second came after his miss was nullified by a holding penalty against Tulsa.

The Gators led 14–0 at the half, but Tulsa came back to score in both the third and fourth quarters. Tulsa kicker Tom Miner missed the second extra point and also missed a short field goal, and Florida held on for a 14–13 win. Florida rushed for 233 yards as Hall went for 94 and Casares for 86. Florida won the game despite losing four fumbles to Tulsa. It was the first of nine Gator Bowl games for the Florida program.

# 48 Rex Grossman

The quarterback sat back in his chair. He wore a three-day beard and a layer of blubber. If he was wearing a sweatshirt that said "COLLEGE," you might have mistaken him for John Belushi. "It's my winter fat," Rex Grossman said when asked about his appearance.

That was Grossman in a nutshell. He enjoyed the college experience and especially enjoyed the offseasons in Gainesville. But when it was time to play, he was one of the best quarterbacks to play at a school known for its quarterbacks. Grossman was a high school star in Bloomington, Indiana, and the *USA Today* Player of the Year. But he wasn't recruited by Florida; it was the other way around.

Grossman and his parents, Dan and Maureen, made a tour of some of the universities they thought might be right for Rex. One of them was Florida. By total coincidence Steve Spurrier happened to be in the office that day. "I was in there about 11:00, and someone came by and said there was a quarterback from Indiana out there who wanted to see me," Spurrier said. "I'd never heard of him to tell the truth. We went and had lunch at the cafeteria, and then I watched his tape that he had brought. He could throw it. He was a player. So I offered him right there. And a week or two later, he called and said he was coming."

Grossman redshirted as a freshman and was the third-string quarterback behind Jesse Palmer and Brock Berlin in 2000. But after a loss at Mississippi State, Spurrier decided to give Grossman a chance. He and Palmer split time, and the Gators were good enough to win the SEC East. "We went to FSU at the end of the year, and they were really good," Spurrier said. "Jesse had a bad game, so I decided to let Rex start the SEC Championship Game."

Grossman was the MVP of the game as Florida beat Auburn 28–6.

The following year Grossman and Berlin were expected to battle in the preseason for the starting job. But it wasn't close. Grossman was clearly the better quarterback and ended up being the starter. He put together one of the best years in Florida history, throwing for 3,896 yards and 34 touchdowns. He barely lost the 2001 Heisman Trophy to Eric Crouch, finishing 62 points behind the Nebraska quarterback in part because of Florida's late-season loss to Tennessee.

During that 2001 season, Grossman set the school record for passing yards in a game with 464 against LSU. "On one play in the game, he was supposed to hit the tight end on a drag route, but he was covered," said Noah Brindise, the former Florida quarterback who was a graduate assistant on the team. "Rex knew Jabar Gaffney was running a clear-out route down the right sidelines. He couldn't see him, but he knew he was supposed to be there so he just threw it and hit him in stride. That was Rex."

During the week of the Orange Bowl, Grossman and some of his teammates missed a curfew. As a result Grossman did not start. Instead he was inserted in the second quarter. He threw for 248 yards and three touchdowns as Florida rolled 56–23.

But two days later while eating lunch with his dad in the Bahamas, Grossman caught a glimpse of a television set that showed Spurrier had resigned. He was floored and even more stunned when the Gators hired Ron Zook. Grossman was ready to turn pro, even though the news he received from the NFL was that he might not be a first-round pick. Zook's first job as the Florida coach was to re-recruit his quarterback.

Assured that Zook would run a wide-open offense under new offensive coordinator Ed Zaunbrecher, Grossman decided to return for his junior season. But it wasn't a happy marriage. Grossman sometimes would mistakenly call out audibles from the Spurrier offense instead of the new one. The offense was up and down as was the UF season. Grossman had some big games—at Tennessee in the rain and against Georgia—but he also threw 17 interceptions.

But when Grossman left Florida, the kid who wasn't recruited by the Gators finished as the third-most efficient passer in SEC history.

# 49 Visit the Adam's Rib Co. Ceiling Mural

To expand his business, he found the perfect building. The ceiling was just a bonus.

When Adam Brewer began shopping around to find a second location for Adam's Rib Co. in Gainesville, he finally settled on a building on SW 13ᵗʰ Street filled with history. It was the site of the original Joe's Deli where so many students through the years had stuffed their faces with oversized subs and prepared for big games with kegs of beer.

Joe's began business in 1975, and two other stores opened, but the original closed in 2007, ending the legacy. It sat there vacant for four years, and everyone thought the next owner would bulldoze the small restaurant. But Brewer liked the building and—while he knew it would need refurbishing—there was the bonus.

In 1985 Joe's Deli owner Bill Reichardt had commissioned artist Jeff Dreisin to paint an orange-and-blue Sistine Chapel on the ceiling as a way of honoring Florida's 1984 football team. That squad won Florida's first SEC title, though the SEC later stripped it.

The ceiling at Joe's Deli (and now Adam's Rib Co.) is unique in that there are panels of varying heights. Dreisin used each panel as a way to illustrate each game from the 9–1–1 season. Each panel had an alligator dressed in full UF uniform tangling with the uniformed mascot of the opponent and displayed the score of the game. "Jeff's brother worked for me at Joe's Deli as a delivery man," Reichardt said. "I came up with the idea when I saw the panels the way they were. It took Jeff, who was a nurse at Shands Hospital, six months to do it. He had his brother modeling for him as he was painting."

Joe's Deli was a landmark place in Gainesville until it closed. When Adam's Rib Co. started to move in, Brewer began looking for Dreisin to touch up the masterpiece. He could never find him, but one of the builders working on the building knew an artist in Gainesville, and Jonathan Wygand preserved the ceiling. "It was in pretty bad shape, but we just thought it would be a good addition to the store," Brewer said. "Everyone knows the history behind it. It speaks for itself."

Brewer had Wygand add a tribute to the 2008 national title team in one of the open frames. It shows Tim Tebow running the football with the BCS insignia also painted on the panel. Adam's definitely has a Gator theme that goes behind the ceiling. The booths are blue with orange trim, and the walls are covered with memorabilia. Among the more notable items:

- A flag from The PLAYERS Championship signed by Danny Wuerffel and Will Muschamp
- A large poster of an artist's rendition of Steve Spurrier
- Footballs signed by different players and one signed by Urban Meyer
- A framed salute to Florida's back-to-back basketball championships
- Several preserved Gators heads
- Assorted framed pictures of Florida athletes in action

Adam's Rib serves hundreds of meals to Gator athletes and caters UF's scholar-athlete dinner twice a year.

# 50 A Dwindling Rivalry with the U

As college football increased in popularity, two major schools from the same state naturally became a part of each other's schedules. As a result Florida and Miami faced each other every year from 1938 (with the exception of 1943 when Florida did not field a team) through the 1987 season. Calling it a bitter rivalry would be an understatement, but it's a rivalry that only pops up on occasion now like a meteor flying by the earth. It's not extinct, but sightings are rare.

The two teams are scheduled to play in 2013 in Miami Gardens. According to several sources, there are no plans to play again. Florida has no interest in playing Miami because it helps Miami a lot more than it helps Florida. It generates ticket revenue for the Hurricanes, but Florida will only play six homes games in 2013 because of the Miami game. Also Florida's schedule already includes eight SEC games and Florida State, and the league could go to nine conference games. So Florida doesn't need to play Miami and may never again, but the games were a thing of beauty.

The rivalry really started to heat up in the 1960s. Florida fans will never forget the 1961 game when right-handed Miami quarterback George Mira threw a left-handed touchdown pass to beat Florida. The Hurricanes also spoiled Steve Spurrier's Heisman Trophy season in 1966 with a win in the final regular-season game.

In 1971 the Gator Flop—when Florida intentionally let Miami score, so Gators quarterback John Reaves could augment his passing stats—took the rivalry to new heights. The following season Miami fans traveled to Florida Field and passed out green cards questioning the class of the Florida football program. And Miami fans are still ticked off about Henry Davis' punt return to win the 1975 game when it appeared his knee touched the ground as he fielded the ball.

Florida-Miami was at its best during the 1980s. Charley Pell had the Florida train rolling, and Howard Schnellenberger had declared South Florida to be the "State of Miami." So when they faced off in 1980, it got ugly. Miami rolled to an easy win, but humbling the Gators wasn't enough. Late in the game, Florida students began pelting the Miami bench with different objects. Schellenberger claimed some of them were frozen oranges. So instead of running the clock out at the end of a 28–7 win, Schnellenberger called a timeout and kicked a late field goal to rub it in. He said he didn't regret it because the field goal brought attention to what was happening on his sidelines.

The following year Miami kicker Dan Miller broke Gators' hearts with a 55-yard field goal to win the game with 40 seconds left. In 1982 it was Florida fullback James Jones' turn. He made a one-handed grab of a wobbling Wayne Peace pass for a 17–14 win. Although it appeared Jones actually landed short of the goal line, the officials ruled it a score. "I told [Miami quarterback] Jim Kelly years later that it was good for them they called it a touchdown," Jones said, "because we were going to score anyway, and it gave them more time."

Kelly was one of the Gators' biggest antagonists not only because of his abilities but also because of his hatred of Florida. His favorite T-shirt read, "Gators Eat Boogers." More than once, television reporters asked him to change the shirt before an interview.

In 1983 Florida won the battle but lost the war. The Gators won 28–3 in Gainesville, but the Hurricanes won the national championship. The following year's game was played in Tampa, Florida, and was the first college football game televised live by ESPN. The Gators nearly pulled the upset with a freshman walk-on quarterback named Kerwin Bell, but Miami scored twice late to win 32–20.

Grumbling began to come out of Gainesville. Florida wanted to drop Miami for several reasons, including the ones already mentioned. The Orange Bowl was considered dangerous. Florida's administration grew more and more frustrated not only with the ticket allocation, but also the location of the seats when they traveled to Miami. When the SEC expanded to eight conference games following the 1987 season, Florida dropped Miami from its annual schedule.

Hurricanes fans were quick with the "chicken Gator" cries, but when Steve Spurrier returned to coach Florida in 1990, he said he wanted Miami back on the schedule. Florida's financial needs and conference obligations hadn't changed, however, and the only game between the two schools during Spurrier's time at UF occurred at the Sugar Bowl after the 2000 season. Showing the rivalry was still alive, players scuffled on Bourbon Street during the week of the game.

When the NCAA decided to add a 12th game for college football, Florida and Miami jumped at the chance and played in 2002 and 2003. Miami won both games, rallying from a 33–10 deficit in 2003 to win. Late in that game, the Miami quarterback Brock Berlin, who used to play for UF, did the Gator Chomp and followed it with a throat-slashing gesture.

The two teams played in 2004 in the Chick-fil-A Bowl with Miami beating a Florida team led by interim coach Charlie Strong, following Ron Zook's dismissal. And then in 2008, the two teams played in The Swamp with Florida winning 26–3. It wouldn't be Florida-Miami without some controversy. Late in that game, Florida coach Urban Meyer chose to kick a field goal rather than run the clock out. Miami coach Randy Shannon barely touched Meyer's hand during the postgame handshake. Shannon, a Miami linebacker when the series was played on an annual basis, complained about the field goal and said, "This will help us more than you will ever know."

The statement was less than prophetic. Florida won the national title that season, and Miami fired Shannon two years later.

# 51 Run Through the Tunnel

It's not quite the same. There won't be 90,000 people in the stands, and you won't be suited up. But you can still take the 27 steps from the doors of the football locker room to the start of the grass field where the Gators play. The Swamp is almost always open. Just stay off the grass. They're fussy about that.

Even on gamedays, though, the tunnel isn't really a tunnel. A canvas shading covers the first half of the jog, and then it's a sea of hands and arms reaching for their favorites as the Florida football team enters the field. There is nothing like running through the band and knowing that memories are about to be made. "It's a feeling you really can't describe," said former UF All-American linebacker Mike Peterson. "The more you get it, the more you want it. Those fans greet you like they haven't seen you in years, and they might have seen you last week. I've played in a lot of professional games, but running through the tunnel at The Swamp is the ultimate."

Heisman Trophy winner Danny Wuerffel likened it to the 1988 movie, *Who Framed Roger Rabbit*, which cleverly mixed animation and live action. "It's just like that in that you run out, and all of a sudden, there are all of these colors and all of these sounds coming at you," Wuerffel said. "It's overwhelming, but you never get tired of it."

Florida players have been running out of the tunnel ever since the locker rooms were moved from the southeast corner to the south end zone in the 1980s. The team was introduced by public address announcer Jim Finch whose voice resembled the way Ed McMahon introduced Johnny Carson on *The Tonight Show*. "Heeerrreee come the Gators!" Finch would boom into the microphone as the players ran through the band. After his death in February of 2002, the university has continued to use a taped audio version of Finch's welcome whenever the Gators take the field.

During his playing days, Tim Tebow lived out a dream because he had been to countless Florida games and saw the players run out of the tunnel. "It's special," he said during his senior year. "The most memorable part of it for me isn't running out. I'm always one of the last ones to run out. I see everybody in front of me running out and then I hear the crowd and then I come jogging out. I think that's what's most special—watching the whole team run out, and being behind them and hearing the crowd once they see them run out and then just this roar. That's the best part for me. It's really cool."

Florida has had different variations of the entrance. After the debut of *Alligator* in 1980, the giant mechanical alligator used for the film was donated to the UF school of engineering with the hopes the students could make it walk and lead the team out onto the field. It never happened, but it was rolled onto Florida Field with cheerleaders pulling it by a rope.

Gators cheerleaders now carry large flags spelling out "F-L-O-R-I-D-A" as the team hits the field.

# The School of Announcers

When young James Bates was visiting Gainesville in 1990 to see his father, Jim, who was then Florida's defensive coordinator, he ran into UF swimmer Dara Torres. He asked her what her major was. "Broadcasting," she said.

The high school kid was taken aback. "You can major in broadcasting?" he asked her.

Now as a professional play-by-play man for CBS College Sports Network, Bates is making the most of his ability to talk. He also had a stint on the Mountain West Network and for several years hosted a TV show on a Gainesville cable access station. He is one of many former Florida football players (not to mention former UF Dazzler Erin Andrews) who you can see or hear on the airwaves during college football season. "It's the brand that is Florida," Bates said. "You can love us or you can hate us, but you can't ignore us."

And you can hardly flip on the TV or radio during football season without hearing from a Gator. "We came out of Florida thinking we were a little different," said Kevin Carter, who works for ESPNU. "Coach [Steve] Spurrier made us think we were something special, and we all came out of there with a sense of purpose. Every Gator you know thinks they are a little bit better."

Among those who have made their mark on the broadcasting profession:

- **Jesse Palmer**—The former UF quarterback worked his way up in the business, starting on Canadian television. He now makes up a major part of Saturday's ESPN studio coverage of games. He also does the color for ESPN's Thursday night games. It's ironic that when Palmer was a player at UF, the school hired a speech therapist for him because he called the plays so quickly in the huddle that players had a hard time understanding what he was saying.
- **Cris Collinsworth**—The former UF wide receiver got his start working with Bob Trumpy on radio in Cincinnati where Collinsworth was a member of the Bengals. Eventually Collinsworth was hired by NBC and is now the color commentator for the network's Sunday Night Football games. One of the major faces and voices of the NFL, he also appears on Showtime's *Inside the NFL*.

*Seated on the NBC set with Bob Costas, Cris Collinsworth is one of the many former Florida players to have gone on to great success as a broadcaster.*

- **Chris Doering**—The former UF wide receiver has been the co-host of a radio show in Gainesville for many years and is now also working as a color analyst for ESPN.
- **Kevin Carter**—The former defensive star worked as a guest correspondent for the NFL Network during playoff games while playing for the Tennessee Titans and worked at a Nashville TV station when time would allow. "I did everything I could," he said. After his playing career, he took some time off before deciding to return to work. He was hired by *SEC Gridiron Live* on Fox Sports South in 2011. ESPNU brought him on in 2012 to be an in-studio analyst every Saturday, and Carter is also on myriad

college football shows during the week on ESPN's various networks. "I wanted to find something that was meaningful and fulfilling," he said. "I love college football. I love covering all the teams."

- **Brady Ackerman**—The walk-on at UF has become a popular radio co-host in Gainesville and Ocala, Florida. He is the sideline commentator for the Gator Radio Network and also is a college football analyst for CSS Sports.

- **Chris Leak**—The former Florida quarterback was a frequent guest on football television shows and was a co-host of a college football show on Sirius/XM before joining the UF coaching staff in 2013.

- **Emmitt Smith**—In addition to winning *Dancing With the Stars*, the NFL's all-time leading rusher had a brief stint on ESPN's pregame NFL coverage in 2007 and 2008.

- **Nat Moore**—He served as the color analyst on Florida's re-broadcasts of games on Sun Sports until 2011 and does work on the Miami Dolphins pregame shows.

- **Scot Brantley**—The former linebacker hosts a radio show in Tampa, Florida, and was a color analyst for Florida games on the Gator Radio Network for several years.

- **Lee McGriff**—He served as color analyst on the Gator Radio Network until his son Travis began playing for the Gators. He resumed his role in 2004.

- **Lomas Brown**—One of the best offensive linemen in Florida history, Brown had a long NFL career and earned a Super Bowl ring with the Tampa Bay Buccaneers before moving on to TV. He's a part of several ESPN shows covering the NFL and its different platforms.

Some other Gators players who have dabbled in radio include Noah Brindise, Doug Johnson, Fred Taylor, Shane Matthews, and Fred Weary.

# 53 The Peaks and Valleys of Doug Dickey

The Florida football career of Doug Dickey goes back to his days as a quarterback in Florida's first bowl game. So you would think his return to his alma mater would have been welcomed with open arms, but this was a complicated time on college campuses where students were feeling more empowered and rebellious. The members of the 1969 Florida football team had no idea that a secret deal had been made for Ray Graves to retire after the season and Dickey to replace him.

So when it happened just days after Graves' Gators had beaten Dickey's Tennessee Vols in the Gator Bowl, the players were upset. Graves had been like a father to many of the players, and they wanted a say in who would replace him. Although Graves had done a wonderful job at UF and would stay on as athletic director, he had been unable to get Florida over the hump to win that first SEC championship. Dickey had won two of the three previous SEC crowns at Tennessee. Surely he had what it took to lead the Gators to the promised land.

What followed over the next nine seasons, however, would be teams loaded with talent and potential who never could quite get over the top. Dickey often infuriated the Gators fan base when he would say he wasn't necessarily trying to win as much as he was trying to "avoid losing."

He also started recruiting a different level of player. Graves had opened the door to African American players. Dickey's vision was to continue that while taking Florida from a pro-style offense to an option offense. He brought in some of the greatest players to ever suit up for the Gators, including Wes Chandler, Jimmy DuBose, Scot Brantley, Sammy Green, and Nat Moore. He was the

## Dickey's Biggest Wins

1. **November 3, 1973 at Auburn**—Florida had never won a game at Jordan-Hare Stadium before this one, but Dickey changed quarterbacks and his offense, and the Gators surprised Auburn 12–8.
2. **November 2, 1974 vs. Auburn**—This game demonstrated that Florida football seemed to be headed in the right direction as the Gators hammered the No. 5-ranked Tigers 25–14.
3. **November 7, 1970 vs. Florida at Jacksonville**—Dickey's first Florida-Georgia game was a good one as Florida won 24–17 thanks to a pair of John Reaves-to-Carlos Alvarez touchdown passes.
4. **October 16, 1971 vs. Florida State**—Florida was 0–5 and FSU 5–0, but the Gators pulled off a stunning 17–15 win.
5. **October 7, 1972 at Florida State**—FSU came in ranked 13th but left with a 42–13 beating.

first Florida coach to start a black quarterback when he gave Don Gaffney the ball against Auburn.

But in so many ways, Dickey was the epitome of the Florida problem. He could win big games but not enough of them. Dickey went 7–21–1 against ranked teams. He never won a bowl game at Florida. He won his first seven games against rival Florida State but only won three of nine games against Georgia. It was Georgia that was his Achilles' heel, and the two losses he suffered to the Bulldogs really started the momentum that ended with him being fired after the 1978 season.

The loaded 1975 team featured Gaffney as a senior and a backfield full of big guys who could run. The Gators lost only once during the season heading into the Georgia game, a controversial 8–7 loss in Raleigh, North Carolina, to Lou Holtz's N.C. State team. But Dickey played it close to the vest against Georgia, holding on to a 7–3 lead for much of the game. Georgia completed an 80-yard pass late in the game to win it.

The following year Florida was up 27–13 and appeared headed for a big SEC win. Georgia scored and Dickey, fearing the Bulldogs had the momentum, went for a fourth-and-1 at his own 29-yard line in the third quarter. The play was stuffed and Georgia never looked back in winning 41–27. The play has been known ever since as "Fourth-and-Dumb." In 1977 Dickey had a backfield that was so speedy it was called the "Woosh-bone." The Gators had 10 players who would end up being drafted after the season, but that team went 6–4–1. Especially tough to take was a 37–9 thumping by FSU in Gainesville for Bobby Bowden's first win against the Gators.

The next year Florida lost three of its first four, and the move was on to get rid of Dickey. Before the season-ending game against Miami, someone painted "Dump Dickey" in big letters on Florida's artificial turf. By Wednesday the school did just that, though it allowed him to coach the finale. Florida lost and finished the season 4–7.

# 54 See the *GameDay* Crew

ESPN's popular pregame college football show has taken on a life of its own with Chris Fowler, Lee Corso, Kirk Herbstreit, and Desmond Howard manning the desk at different college campuses around America. And the chances are good that if you follow the Gators, you'll get the opportunity to see the show in person...or at least be in the background while they broadcast.

Since the show began going live from the sites of big college games, no school has been involved in more *GameDay* productions than the University of Florida. UF was also the first school to have

## *GameDay* Appearances

Here's a look at each *GameDay* appearance at Florida games:

**1995—Gainesville** Florida 35, Florida State 24
**1996—Tempe, Arizona (Fiesta Bowl)** Nebraska 62, Florida 24
**1996—Knoxville, Tennessee** Florida 35, Tennessee 29
**1996—Tallahassee, Florida** Florida State 24, Florida 21
**1997—New Orleans, Louisiana (Sugar Bowl)** Florida 52, Florida State 20
**1997—Gainesville** Florida 33, Tennessee 20
**1997—Baton Rouge, Louisiana** LSU 28, Florida 21
**1997—Auburn, Alabama** Florida 24, Auburn 10
**1997—Gainesville** Florida 32, Florida State 29
**1999—Gainesville** Florida 23, Tennessee 21
**1999—Jacksonville, Florida** Florida 30, Georgia 14
**1999—Gainesville** Florida State 30, Florida 23
**2000—Knoxville, Tennessee** Florida 27, Tennessee 23
**2000—Tallahassee, Florida** Florida State 30, Florida 7
**2001—Columbia, South Carolina** Florida 54, South Carolina 17
**2001—Gainesville** Tennessee 34, Florida 32
**2002—Gainesville** Miami 41, Florida 16
**2002—Knoxville, Tennessee** Florida 30, Tennessee 13
**2002—Jacksonville, Florida** Florida 20, Georgia 13
**2003—Gainesville** Florida State 38, Florida 34
**2005—Jacksonville, Florida** Florida 14, Georgia 10
**2006—Gainesville** Florida 23, LSU 10
**2006—Auburn, Alabama** Auburn 27, Florida 17
**2007—Glendale, Arizona (BCS National Championship Game)** Florida 41, Ohio State 14
**2007—Baton Rouge, Louisiana** LSU 28, Florida 24
**2007—Lexington, Kentucky** Florida 45, Kentucky 37
**2008—Gainesville** Florida 26, Miami 3
**2008—Atlanta (SEC Championship Game)** Florida 31, Alabama 20
**2009—Miami Gardens, Forida (BCS National Championship Game)** Florida 24, Oklahoma 14
**2009—Baton Rouge, Louisiana** Florida 13, LSU 3
**2009—Gainesville** Florida 37, Florida State 10
**2009—Atlanta (SEC Championship Game)** Alabama 32, Florida 13
**2012—College Station, Texas** Florida 20, Texas A&M 17
**2012—Knoxville, Tennessee** Florida 37, Tennessee 20
**2012—Gainesville** Florida 14, LSU 6

*GameDay* on campus for a spring game (in 2008). *GameDay* has been at a Florida game 35 times, and the Gators have a respectable 24–11 record in those games.

The show began on ESPN in 1987 as a studio pregame show and started going to the campuses in 1993 when Florida and Notre Dame were playing in South Bend, Indiana. Since then in only five seasons has Florida not been featured—1994, 1998, 2004, 2010, and 2011. Florida is now 8–4 when *GameDay* has been in Gainesville. The Gators have their most *GameDay* wins against Tennessee with six (one loss) and have never lost to Georgia when *GameDay* is on the scene.

In 2012 three Florida games were featured on *GameDay*. The Gators had the most appearances of any school when four Gators games were included in 1997. When the crew is in Gainesville, it sets up in the north end zone, and fans show up early with signs that can be seen in the background. The Gators cheerleaders also perform behind the set, and every so often, you'll see a female cheerleader raised into the air to do the Gator Chomp.

When he picked Ohio State to beat Penn State in 1996, Corso began donning head gear of the mascot for the team he is picking to win. If he pulls out Albert's head to pick the Gators, he receives the loudest roar of the day from the UF fans in attendance.

# 55 A Muddy Loss

Florida football didn't have a lot to crow about in its early years, but one of its best ever teams played in 1928 with Charlie Bachman as the coach. Bachman, a former Notre Dame player, took over the

## Could've Been Contenders

The 1928 team was one of the best ever at UF but ended the season without any kind of championship. Here are five of the best Gators teams to miss out on a championship.

**2001**—Steve Spurrier's last team lost two games by five points and steamrolled Maryland in the Orange Bowl, but LSU won the SEC.

**2009**—Tim Tebow's senior year produced a 12–0 regular season, but a loss in the SEC Championship Game to Alabama ruined it.

**1969**—One bad day on the plains of Auburn was followed by a tie against Georgia. The Super Sophs were denied.

**2012**—Will Muschamp's second team could have been playing for the national title, but six turnovers against Georgia killed the Gators.

**1975**—This awesome wishbone team lost two regular season games by four points and fell short of SEC title again.

**Note:** *This list does not include the 1984, 1985, and 1990 teams that won SEC championships but were denied their places in history because of NCAA sanctions.*

program that year and would coach through 1932. His 1928 team was his best, an unstoppable force that embarrassed teams and set the national record for points scored in a season with 336.

The Gators were 8–0 when they traveled to Knoxville to face national power Tennessee, coached by legendary Robert Neyland. The legend goes that the Rose Bowl, the only bowl game played that year, was on the line for the winner. But the winner did not go, and even at 9–0, Florida's chances of going to its first bowl game were not set in stone by any means. In his pregame speech, Bachman claimed to have a telegram in his hands that proved UF would be invited with a win. But Georgia Tech—9–0 and Southern Conference champs heading into bowl season—ended up playing California, and Bachman later admitted he knew Tech would be invited. Still the stage was set for a dramatic game between the Gators and Vols.

Florida had its "Phantom Four" backfield of Carl Bumbraugh, Rainey Cawthon, Clyde Crabtree, and Royce Goodbread. Bumbraugh had scored three touchdowns in two minutes in a rout of Auburn that season. The Gators also had their first All-American in end Dale Van Sickel, and a speedy running back named Red Bethea. No slouch, Tennessee had an 8–0–1 record and a defense that had produced five shutouts. Bobby Dodd, who went on to become one of college football's great coaches, quarterbacked the Vols.

When Florida showed up for the game, the Gators were surprised to find the field wet and muddy on a cold day. Conspiracy theorists alleged that Tennessee watered the field overnight. Only a light rain fell during the previous evening. There was also the theory that the field froze and then thawed out. Whatever really happened, the muddy field slowed down the speedy Gators. They missed a pair of extra points and ended up losing 13–12. Florida wouldn't play Tennessee again for 18 years.

# 56 Mick Hubert

Florida has enjoyed a lot of success on the athletic fields since 1990. Maybe Mick Hubert deserves some of the credit; his tenure certainly coincides with the best of times at Florida.

Hubert came to Florida in 1989 as the play-by-play announcer for football, basketball, and baseball and walked into a mess. In his first year on the job, Florida fired its football and basketball coaches and was dealing with an NCAA investigation. "My wife would pick up the paper every morning, and there would be talk

## The History of Gator Announcers

Red Barber was a Florida student and a part-time janitor when he decided to become a broadcaster. Although Barber made his name doing New York Yankees games, he started out doing Florida football games in 1930.

It wasn't a full-time job. Barber broadcast a game here and there for a few years until he graduated. After Barber, Dan Riss did some play-by-play until he left for a job in Cincinnati. Dave Russell was the play-by-play man in 1939, and WRUF, the university station, hired a student named Otis Boggs to be the co-announcer.

Russell left for Dallas the next year, and Boggs would occupy the play-by-play chair until he retired in 1981. During that time Gators fans relied on the radio to find out how their Gators were doing because so few games were televised. Boggs became synonymous with Florida football. After Boggs retired, David Steele took over the role of the play-by-play man. He did the games from 1982 to 1989 when he left to be the voice of the Orlando Magic.

of a death penalty," he said. "She'd go to work in tears, wondering what we got into."

But since then Florida has had a string of championships, and Hubert has been there to call them all. During one stretch in 2005 and 2006, he called Florida's first ever SEC tournament title in basketball, its first appearance in the College World Series final, its first basketball national title, and its second football championship. "I'm the luckiest guy in the world," he said. "I don't think any other announcers have been able to do that."

A graduate of Illinois State, Hubert was working at WHIO in Dayton when a friend told him about the job opening up at Florida. Hubert knew little about the Gators but put together a tape to send to UF. A few days later, he was flown in for an interview. After returning to Dayton, he was sound asleep one morning when the phone rang. It was then-Florida athletic director Bill Arnsparger. "How'd you like to be a Gator?" Arnsparger asked.

Hubert began calling games during the 1989 season. In the middle of the season, Florida fired Galen Hall. "We'd done the TV show after we got back from LSU, and the next day I'm watching the TV, and this crawl comes across that he had been let go," Hubert said. "I had also gotten to know [basketball coach] Norm Sloan, and a few weeks later he was fired."

But the good times were on the horizon. Hubert has called four national football title games, four Final Fours, and six College World Series. His signature phrase is to exclaim, "Oh my!" after a big play. Hubert is quick to admit he stole the phrase from NBC's Dick Enberg. "Steve Spurrier was at a golf outing, and he told Enberg that there was a guy back in Gainesville who was using that phrase," Hubert said. "Dick told him that was okay because he had stolen the phrase from a guy in the 1940s."

Although he treasures all of the championships he has called, Hubert's favorite broadcast came in a regular season game in Lexington, Kentucky, in 1993 when Florida scored the winning touchdown with seven seconds to play. His "Doering's got a touchdown!" (in reference to Chris Doering's reception) is a favorite among Gators fans and established Hubert as the man on radio. The game was only on pay-per-view, which was primitive at the time, so a majority of UF fans listened to Hubert's broadcast. "You don't get a chance to call it a second time," he said. "In 1989 I was the new guy. In 1990 I was still the guy who replaced David Steele. In 1991 I was Mark Herbert. In 1992 I was Mick Herbert. But after that game, everyone knew who I was. Keith Jackson played the clip on ABC the next week. Lee McGriff [the color analyst] told me he had never seen me like that. He said, 'You were standing up. You had me backed against the wall. You were coming out of yourself, going nuts.' It was just a special moment."

Another of his favorite moments was calling Florida's victory against Florida State in the 1997 Sugar Bowl when Florida won its first national championship. He also called the two BCS National Championship games under Urban Meyer. "It's a miracle," he said. "I thank God all the time. I have a friend, Tommy Waters, who built both of my houses in Gainesville. He tells me all the time that before I got to Florida, there were so many, 'Wait 'til next years.' And when I got here, they started winning championships."

Hubert has worked with three different analysts on the radio broadcasts of Florida football. Lee McGriff had been working with David Steele and continued with Hubert until 1994 when McGriff's sons became old enough to start playing college football. James Jones, a former Florida running back, took over from 1994 to 1996. Former linebacker Scot Brantley held the job from 1997 to 2003. Then McGriff stepped back into the booth.

## 57 Chris Leak

For Chris Leak getting to the mountaintop was not the big surprise it was to the rest of the college football nation. It was expected.

From the time he signed with the University of Florida, he had no doubt his career would end the way it did—with confetti rain and a crystal ball trophy. "When I committed to Florida, the mission was to bring Florida back to prominence," Leak said. "After the dust settled, it was mission accomplished. This was what I came to the University of Florida to do—win a national title, get back to dominance."

In his final game as a Gator, Leak was named the Most Valuable Player of the BCS National Championship Game against Ohio State. He was flawless in the game and even though a lot of the attention went to his backup quarterback, Leak never wavered in his commitment to getting Florida back among the elite teams in America.

Whether it was bringing water to his teammates during voluntary workouts or leading in the weight room, Leak's style was not rah-rah, but it was effective. "It was crucial," Urban Meyer said. "We were talking the other day about the example he set in the weight room."

Meyer inherited Leak along with 20 other starters on that 2006 national championship team, but he also helped mold the quarterback into a more vocal player.

The Chris Leak story goes all the way back to the eighth grade when he committed to play for Wake Forest where his brother, C.J., had signed to play quarterback. When Wake Forest fired coach Jim Caldwell, the school fell off the Leak radar. By the time Leak was ready to choose a college, the *Parade* All-American and one of the top recruits in the country had led Charlotte (North Carolina) Independence High to three straight state titles.

Ron Zook, the coach at Florida, wrote the Leaks a letter that spelled out his plan for Chris. "A lot of it was predicated on whether or not Rex Grossman came back for his senior year," Leak said. "But it showed that I could trust him."

When Leak made his official visit to Florida, he went alone because his father, Curtis, didn't want to influence him. "Rex was my host," Leak said. "I went to the Auburn game where he threw the winning touchdown in overtime. The whole experience in The Swamp was overwhelming. I call it falling in love. I really fell in love with the university."

Leak chose Florida, a major coup for Zook. His plan was for Leak to play in every game as a freshman. As it turned out, he was *starting* by the fifth game of the 2003 season. His first two seasons came with more highs and lows than the stock market. Leak led his team to a win in Baton Rouge, Louisiana, as a freshman, and

LSU would go on to win the national title that year. But the Gators would lose at home to Ole Miss and Florida State and then in the Outback Bowl to Iowa.

Zook was fired midway through Leak's sophomore season after a loss to Mississippi State. But the Gators beat FSU in Tallahassee on the night they dedicated the field to Bobby Bowden. "We were in a constant state of flux, trying to put a team together," Leak said. "We were really young, doing on-the-job training. I don't want to say the mistakes were expected, but they were natural for a young team."

Enter Meyer. Right after he got the job, Meyer called Leak, who was at the SEC Championship Game to support his brother C.J. (who had transferred to Tennessee). "He told me they were going to build the team around me," Leak said. "And he told me the team was going to go as far as I took them."

One of Meyer's goals was to get Leak to be more vocal. The quarterback had communicated mostly by hand signals in the previous offense. "I was only 19 so I was still a teenager trying to become a man," Leak said. "He was going to give me the keys to the car. I felt like I had always been a leader, but you always have to be ready to take a step up to the next level."

That team went 9–3 despite numerous injuries to the wide receiver corps. Meyer put together one of the best classes ever at Florida the following year, and it included a quarterback named Tim Tebow. "Tim was mature beyond his years," Leak said. "But he was a guy who would listen. Our relationship was not adversarial like a lot of people thought."

Tebow made major contributions to the 2006 Gators team, but it was still Leak's team. The Gators lost only at Auburn that season and rolled into the national title game as a big underdog. But for Leak, winning that game was hardly a surprise. "To me, it was expected," he said. "The journey of getting there was what stood out for me."

All of the workouts, all of the tough losses, and all of the criticism for sliding instead of taking the extra yard, it all became worth it in the end. "When I left Florida, I wanted people to think of Chris Leak as a guy who wanted to serve others," he said, "that I was unselfish."

Leak finished his career by serving up 11,213 passing yards, the most of any quarterback in the history of the school. And he finished as a national championship quarterback.

# 58 Eat Chiappini's Boiled Peanuts

For a lot of families, munching on boiled peanuts at some point in the day is a Gators gameday tradition. The tasty treat is consumed everywhere. They may be too messy for the car, but the smell of the southern delicacy also can be too intoxicating to resist. Tailgating areas are strewn with the soft shells of the soaked peanuts, and you step on dozens of them while shuffling to your seat at The Swamp.

Although tailgates have become more sophisticated with time, there is nothing complicated about boiled peanuts. The salty snack remains a staple for Florida football games—and a Chiappini's tradition. Stands on the side of the road—no matter which direction you come from when arriving for a Florida football game—sell the boiled delicacies.

But Chiappini's Gulf Station has its own special ambience. A brick building located where State Roads 21 and 26 intersect also marks the intersection of four counties—Alachua, Bradford, Clay, and Putnam. Chiappini's is located in Melrose, a lake town where many Gainesville residents either have summer homes or have moved permanently. (Urban Meyer still has a home on Melrose Lake, and former Florida quarterback Doug Johnson lives close by.)

Chiappini's—a brick convenience store and gas station still run by the original owners' grandsons, Mark and Rob—was built in the 1930s and has been the hangout for decades for anyone wanting to talk politics or sports. It has its regulars (think *The Andy Griffith Show*), but for a lot of Gator fans, it's only a stop during the handful of times a year they visit on their way to games.

Melrose is between Crescent Beach on Florida's east coast—where so many Gainesville residents vacation and students play hooky—and the Florida campus. For residents of St. Augustine or Palatka to the east, it has become a tradition to visit Chiappini's to load up on boiled peanuts and stop for one final bathroom break. Inhabitants of nearby Keystone Heights stop at Chiappini's for supplies before making the 19-mile trip into town.

It's not just the convenience of a place right on the way to the stadium that attracts Florida fans. It's the tradition. For some Chiappini's is where their father took them—and his father before that. The aroma of the gas station will bring back memories. Then you can turn the radio to the pregame show as the road thickens with fans riding in cars decorated with Gator flags and magnetic stickers.

And now you have some boiled peanuts for the rest of the ride.

# 59 Will Muschamp

The little boy used to imagine that he would play in the big stadium just a few blocks away. He wanted to be Tony Lilly, the hard-hitting safety from the early 1980s, and wear that orange jersey and hear the announcer say in that deep voice, "Heeerrreee come the Gators!"

But it wasn't meant to be for the young boy who grew up in Gainesville. A broken leg hurt his scholarship chances, and when he went to Steve Spurrier's office to see about being a walk-on, nobody was around. Instead Will Muschamp went to Georgia, earned a scholarship, and became a hard-hitting safety in his own right. He wouldn't fulfill his Gator dreams until he became the head coach.

When Urban Meyer stepped down (this time for good) following the 2010 season, Florida athletic director Jeremy Foley once again began a search to find a coach to follow a legend. He had struck out with the hiring of Ron Zook to replace Steve Spurrier but again targeted a defensive coordinator with a reputation as a great recruiter and no head coaching experience.

When he woke up a few days after Meyer's resignation, Foley had a bunch of names rattling around in his head, but the name Will Muschamp stood out. Muschamp had a lot of things that Foley wanted. He could recruit, he knew the SEC after stints at Auburn and LSU, and he knew the traditions and history at Florida. Muschamp had moved to Gainesville when he was eight years old and attended Oak Hall High, often walking to Florida Field to watch the Gators play.

Foley also knew that Muschamp was a hot commodity. Not only was he the officially designated coach-in-waiting at Texas where Muschamp was the defensive coordinator, but he also had turned down several offers to be the head coach at BCS schools, including Tennessee.

If he moved on from Texas, Muschamp was going to wait for the right job. "I know the Gator Nation is going to have high expectations," Muschamp said at his introductory press conference. "I expect to win. We're not on a five-year plan."

Florida fans expecting a home run hire were a bit put off and wondered if Florida had hired another Zook. "I probably heard that

*Known as "Coach Boom," fiery coach Will Muschamp exhorts his defense during Florida's 20–17 win against Texas A&M in 2012.* (AP Images)

during the offseason," Muschamp said. And things didn't get better during a stormy first season. After starting off 4–0, Muschamp lost his quarterback John Brantley against Alabama. Florida offensive coordinator Charlie Weis had put everything on Brantley, and Florida's two freshmen quarterbacks weren't ready. Losses to LSU and Auburn followed.

Brantley returned with a heavily taped ankle against Georgia and led the Gators to a 17–3 lead. But that lead unraveled into a

## Coach Boom

His reputation coming to Florida was of a coach who wears his emotions on his sleeve. Will Muschamp earned the nickname "Coach Boom" while at Texas. Would he conduct himself differently as head coach? "I'm going to be myself," he said.

There have been plenty of examples, showing that he hasn't changed much.

- During a 2011 game against Auburn, the sideline microphones picked up Muschamp, saying some unpleasant things to the officials following a Chris Rainey muffed punt. Muschamp apologized the following week for his language.
- After the win at Texas A&M in 2012, Muschamp went off on reporters. A week earlier Florida had struggled against Bowling Green, and Muschamp was criticized by fans and media alike. "I got killed for last week, but there's a reason why we did it," Muschamp said, his voice getting louder and louder in a cramped room at Kyle Field. "We needed to play that way—in order to play that way this week—in this ballgame. It's a long season! When they start having one-game seasons, then we'll start doing everything we can do. We'll put everything we can into one game, so we can win one game and all be really, really happy at the end! But I like to look at it as a 12-week season, and we've got to do what we've got to do to improve our football team to win football games!"
- At halftime of the 2012 game against South Carolina, Muschamp was approached by the Gator Radio Network's Brady Ackerman for their weekly two-question briefing. Muschamp answered Ackerman's question and then began shouting into the microphone, "We have to overcome the adversity on the field!" Muschamp barked. Coach Boom wasn't happy with a lack of holding calls in the Gamecocks. Ackerman later said he didn't feel the need to ask a second question.

24–20 loss—Florida's fourth straight. Losses at South Carolina and at home against Florida State left Florida with a 6–6 record. The Gators beat Ohio State in the Gator Bowl to avoid their first losing season since 1979.

But between that loss to FSU and the Gator Bowl, two things happened to help Muschamp. First, Urban Meyer took the Ohio State job, leaving the perception that he had abandoned a sinking ship at UF. That gave Muschamp a longer leash with the fans. And during the practices for the bowl game, Muschamp decided that he couldn't worry about injuries any more despite his depleted roster. The Gators' physical practices set the tone for 2012.

Florida's schedule for 2012 was hardly ideal. They had to travel to Texas A&M for the Aggies' first ever SEC game. The atmosphere was electric, but Florida prevailed over A&M. The next week they went to Knoxville, Tennessee, and beat the Volunteers. A special season built around defense and the running game continued with wins over LSU and South Carolina. A loss to Georgia—when Florida committed six turnovers—was the only thing that kept the Gators from playing for the national title in Muschamp's second season.

Although a Sugar Bowl loss at the end of the season was a letdown, Florida was clearly moving in the right direction. "We overachieved in 2012, and it was a great season," Muschamp said. "I like where we're going."

# The Overtime Era

When college football began to play overtime games in 1996, Gator Nation wondered when it would come into play for a Florida team.

In its long history, Florida had played 40 tie games, though none of them had the same kind of impact as the overtime games that UF would play. There have been five, and each has been spectacular:

### September 20, 1998 at Tennessee

Florida went into the game ranked second in the country. Tennessee was No. 6 but had home-field advantage. The Gators dominated the game but couldn't hold onto the ball. With a crowd of 107,653 watching in Neyland Stadium and millions more on CBS, Florida alternated quarterback Doug Johnson and Jesse Palmer on every other play—much the way Steve Spurrier had in a win over Florida State the year before.

But this time the Gators turned it over seven times, including a Terry Jackson fumble at the goal line. Tennessee linebacker Al Wilson caused three Florida fumbles, and the Vols led 17–10 until Palmer hit Travis McGriff with a 70-yard touchdown pass. The two teams went to overtime, and Tennessee appeared to be in trouble when the Vols were called for holding. But a 10-yard scramble by UT quarterback Tee Martin set up a 41-yard field goal by Jeff Hall.

Florida moved into position for a 32-yard field goal to tie it, but Collins Cooper hooked the kick, and Tennessee fans spilled onto the field. The Volunteers, who had not beaten UF since 1992, went on to win the national title in 1998.

### October 2, 1999 vs. Alabama

Florida entered the game on a 30-game winning streak at home, and Alabama had lost to Louisiana Tech just two weeks earlier. But this would turn into one of the most unreal games at The Swamp.

Florida couldn't stop Alabama running back Shaun Alexander, who scored four times, and Alabama couldn't stop Florida wide receiver Darrell Jackson, who scored three times. But it was a late fumbled punt by Jackson that allowed Alabama a chance to score the tying points. Alexander's 13-yard run on fourth down sent the game to extra time.

Florida scored, but the usually reliable Jeff Chandler pushed the extra point wide to the right. On Alabama's first play, Alexander went 25 yards for a touchdown. The extra point was also missed by Alabama, but a UF offside penalty gave Alabama a second chance, and that kick was true, giving the Tide the 40–39 win. Alabama would beat Florida again that year, winning 34–7 in the SEC Championship Game.

### October 19, 2002 vs. Auburn

In Ron Zook's first season as Florida's coach, the Gators appeared to have clinched a big win over the Tigers. The Gators were up 23–7 in the fourth quarter, and Auburn running back Cadillac Williams was out of the game.

But behind quarterback Jason Campbell and backup tailback Ronnie Brown, the Tigers rallied. They scored twice, and each time converted the two-point conversion. On third down in overtime, Florida quarterback Rex Grossman hit Taylor Jacobs with a 25-yard pass to the back of the end zone. Campbell was sacked from behind by Clint Mitchell and fumbled away the ball to the Gators, and UF won 30–23.

### November 5, 2005 vs. Vanderbilt

This was one of Vandy's best teams with future Chicago Bears, Jay Cutler and Earl Bennett at quarterback and wideout, respectively. It was one of the best offensive performances for Urban Meyer's first Florida team, but the Gators couldn't stop the Commodores.

The game went to overtime tied at 35, and both teams scored touchdowns in the first overtime. Vandy coach Bobby Johnson later revealed he planned to go for two, but Bennett was flagged for unsportsmanlike conduct for giving a slight shoulder wiggle after his score, and Vandy had to kick the extra point from 15 yards back.

## Famous Two-Point Conversions

The two-point conversion was voted into college football in 1958, and since that time, it has become a big part of Gators football lore. Some of them worked; some of them did not. Here are the five most famous two-point plays in UF history:

1. The backdrop for the third game of Ray Graves' Florida coaching career was a father-son battle in 1960. Georgia Tech was coached by Bobby Dodd and his son, Bobby Jr., was the Florida quarterback. The No. 10-ranked Yellow Jackets were the favorites in Gainesville that day, but the game turned into a punting battle as Florida stayed close. Tech had a late score on a 73-yard drive to take a 17–10 lead, and Florida had one chance. The Gators drove 85 yards and scored on a fourth-down play when quarterback Larry Libertore pitched to halfback Lindy Infante, who snuck it inside the pylon with 33 seconds to play.

   One of the most famous pictures in Gator history is of Graves holding two fingers in the air on the sideline. Florida would go for the win. Libertore faked a run and then flipped the ball to Jon MacBeth in the end zone for the winning conversion.

2. Florida trailed Georgia 10–3 late in the 1973 game in Jacksonville, Florida, and the Gators offense was struggling. But quarterback Don Gaffney engineered a drive that gave them a chance. His touchdown pass to a leaping Lee McGriff made it 10–9. McGriff was so elated he threw the ball in the air, and UF was penalized on the kickoff. But first there would be the two-point try. "I wanted the ball again," McGriff said. "And I was open."

   But Gaffney instead found tight end Hank Foldberg Jr. in the end zone for the winning points.

3. Because the tragic events of 9/11 forced changes to the schedule, the Florida-Tennessee game was played at the end of the 2001 season with a berth in the SEC Championship Game on the line.

Florida could not contain running back Travis Stephens
of Tennessee and found itself trailing 34–26 late in the game.
But the Gators drove down the field, scoring on a short Rex
Grossman pass to Carlos Perez.

Florida had no choice but to go for two. The play was
supposed to be a pass to Taylor Jacobs, but Grossman
thought he saw Jabar Gaffney open. Instead Tennessee
knocked the pass away, and the Vols went to Atlanta.

4. In the aftermath of the 1966 Sugar Bowl, Florida fans on
   Bourbon Street carried signs that read, "7x3=21."

   Perhaps the Gators should have relied on this basic
   arithmetic. Steve Spurrier had rallied his team from down 20–0
   against Missouri with three touchdowns. But Florida went for
   two all three times. The second thwarted attempt came on a
   fake extra point. On the third try, Spurrier missed, and Florida
   suffered a defeat that was difficult to stomach for the Gators
   faithful.

5. Unbeaten Florida went to Tampa, Florida, in 1969 to face
   Tulane, thinking it would be a cakewalk. The Blue Wave
   had yet to win a game while UF was 3–0 and ranked 12th in
   the nation. But it took a late drive for the Gators to have an
   opportunity to win the game. After Tommy Durrance scored,
   Graves decided to go for two. "I had been out for most of
   the series with cramps," wide receiver Carlos Alvarez said.
   "They put me in the slot, and I ran an out route. We figured
   they would be in man coverage, but they were in a zone. John
   Reaves threw a beautiful, beautiful pass with no margin for
   error because the defensive back broke on it and missed it by
   a foot."

   Alvarez made the catch, and Florida escaped with an 18–17
   win. "I remember Coach Graves telling us before the game we
   were going to lose because we weren't focused," Alvarez said.
   "After the game there was no celebration. It was more of a
   relief."

In the second overtime, Florida scored on a pass from Chris Leak to Jemalle Cornelius, and Reggie Lewis picked off a Cutler pass to finally end the game.

### October 30, 2010 vs. Georgia at Jacksonville, Florida

Urban Meyer's last game against Georgia was a doozy as two struggling teams battled to a 31–31 tie in regulation.

On Georgia's first overtime possession, a tipped Aaron Murray pass was picked off by Will Hill. He ran it back for an apparent game-winning score, but replays showed he stepped out on the 3-yard line.

Hill was so winded from the return that he took his pads off on the sideline as Florida went on offense. The Gators moved the ball into position to set up a 37-yard field goal for Chas Henry, who had taken over the kicking duties because of an injury to Caleb Sturgis. Georgia defensive coordinator Todd Grantham grabbed his neck in a choking gesture and uttered curse words at Henry, but Henry calmly nailed the kick and set off a wild celebration for Gators fans.

# 61 Zook's Bad Luck

The night before Florida's game at LSU in 2001, Florida athletic director Jeremy Foley talked to some reporters. They asked him about his "List."

The List was always there in his desk at the University of Florida. It included the names of the coaches he would consider if any of his head coaches left. But on this night, the reporters were curious about the football list. Foley said he was very interested in Bobby Stoops, a former UF defensive coordinator, and Mike

Shanahan, a former UF offensive coordinator. And then he added the name of Ron Zook, which blew everyone away.

Sure enough, Spurrier resigned following the season, and Foley went to work. He talked to Stoops, who decided to remain the Oklahoma coach and turned him down. He went to Denver where Shanahan was coaching the Broncos. "That was a circus," Foley would say later. The media got wind of Foley's visit, and cameras were everywhere he went. But Shanahan passed as well.

That left Zook, who was named defensive coordinator under Steve Spurrier in 1991 before being demoted to special teams coach after the 1993 season. There was no middle ground with Gator fans on Zook. They either loved him—or thought Foley had made a huge mistake. (At the 2005 spring game after Foley had changed coaches, he joked: "That's the first time in three years I've been able to walk through the parking lot without wearing Kevlar.") One fan started a website called FireRonZook.com. And Zook hadn't even coached a game yet.

At his introductory press conference, Zook said over and over again, "I'm not Steve Spurrier." That wasn't what Florida fans wanted to hear. They wanted another Steve Spurrier. Instead they got a career assistant coach who had been demoted by that head coach. Spurrier and Zook went to dinner that night, and Spurrier told the new coach, "You know, they hired you because nobody else would take it."

When Foley offered Zook the job, Zook didn't ask how much it would pay. Instead he asked for a cell phone so he could start recruiting. And he recruited like a maniac. When he left Florida, Zook left behind an amazing array of talent for Urban Meyer. Of the 24 starters in the 2007 BCS National Championship Game, 23 of them were recruited by Zook. But a few things made Zook's career at Florida a short one.

He was following a coach who had won six SEC championships and a national title and changed the culture at Florida.

Under Zook, Florida lost 14 games in three seasons, and he lost more home games in three years than Spurrier did in 12. Zook's personality clashed with boosters and the media and—most famously—a fraternity. Some of Zook's players had been involved in a fight at the Pi Kappa Phi house, and Foley told Zook to go to the house to talk to the fraternity members. According to police reports, Zook became confrontational and said, "I will do anything in my power to take this house down." The story broke just days after Florida had lost a heartbreaker at Tennessee. "If I raised my voice, I apologize," Zook said. "This university deserves to be represented in the right way and in a professional way."

But the final reason for his short tenure was that the guy couldn't catch a break. He had the worst luck. Every time it looked like things were turning around, Florida would suffer an inexplicable loss. As part of Zookluck, the schedule of his first two seasons included Miami, even though Florida hadn't played the Hurricanes since 1987. And this was when Miami was still the college football power. Florida lost both games.

In a 2003 game against Tennessee, the Vols threw a Hail Mary pass at the end of the first half. Of course, it was caught for a touchdown and spurred Tennessee to a victory. While playing Florida State that same year, several Seminole fumbles were not ruled as fumbles, and replays showed a key Florida fumble that was returned for a touchdown shouldn't have been a fumble. Instead running back Ciatrick Fason's knee was down. FSU won in what is now called "The Swindle in The Swamp."

While Florida tried to run out the clock with a one-point lead in a 2004 game at Tennessee, Dallas Baker was flagged for a personal foul for retaliating against a Vols player. But the Tennessee player had hit him first. If that wasn't enough, the officials forgot to restart the clock. Tennessee kicked a field goal to win 30–28 on the last play of the game.

Three hurricanes brushed Gainesville during the summer of 2004, and the last one forced a postponement of the opening game. Since that opener was played during what was supposed to be Florida's open date, the team never had a week off. During the middle of that season, Foley approached Zook in the Florida weight room and told him, "You need to go to the president's house." Zook replied, "Am I in trouble?"

He was. UF president Bernie Machen fired Zook, but Foley had convinced the president to let Zook coach out the year. His last game was a stunning win at Florida State, and Zook was carried off the field on the shoulders of some of his players. During his time at UF, Zook has some remarkable wins. He beat Georgia twice—once when the Bulldogs were unbeaten—won at Tennessee and won at LSU in 2003. The Tigers went on to win the national championship that season.

But the losses were just too plentiful. Zook did not coach in the UF bowl game that year. He accepted the head coaching job at Illinois and stalled Foley on whether he would coach in the Chick-fil-A Bowl against Miami. Foley finally made the decision for him, naming defensive coordinator Charlie Strong the interim coach for the bowl game. During the week several coaches, who were going to Illinois with Zook, wore Illinois shirts at practices. Not surprisingly Florida lost 27–10.

# Gators in the NFL Draft

If there was any more true indication of how much Florida stumbled during the 2011 season when the Gators went 7–6, it was displayed during the NFL Draft.

*Jevon Kearse, who the Tennessee Titans selected with the 16ᵗʰ overall pick in the 1999 NFL Draft, readies to rush the passer during a 24–3 victory against Auburn in 1998.*

## Draft Trivia
### Questions
1. Who was the first Florida player ever taken in the NFL Draft?
2. In what decade did Florida have the most players drafted?
3. Which current NFL team has selected the fewest number of Florida players?
4. Who was the last Florida punter to be selected by an NFL team?
5. In what two years did Florida have three players taken in the first round, the most ever for the school?

**Answers**

1. Walter Mayberry, a running back, went to the Cleveland Rams in the sixth round of the 1938 Draft; 2. In the 1990s Florida had 52 players selected. The 2000 to 2009 decade came close with 50 players taken; 3. The Houston Texans have taken only one player from UF—Jabar Gaffney in 2002 in the second round; 4. Punter Ray Criswell was taken in the fifth round by the Philadelphia Eagles in 1986; 5. Three players (Trace Armstrong, David Williams, and Louis Oliver) were taken in 1989, and three players (Tim Tebow, Joe Haden, and Maurkice Pouncey) were taken in 2010.

In the 1970s, '80s, and '90s, the draft had been a great advertisement for the level of success of Florida's program. During those three decades, 136 Florida players were taken by NFL teams. In the 2012 Draft, only two players were taken, and the highest pick was Jaye Howard in the fourth round. The Gators rebounded in 2013 as eight Gators were selected, the second most ever in a seven-round draft. During every year of a stretch from 1983 to 1991, UF had a player selected in the first round. That's the second longest streak ever for a school. Miami had a 14-year run that went from 1995 to 2008.

Florida has had a first-round pick in 32 NFL Drafts, which is the fifth most of any school. The two most recent were defensive lineman Shariff Floyd (Minnesota Vikings) and safety Matt Elam (Baltimore Ravens) who were taken in the first round of the 2013 Draft. It started with running back Paul Duhart, who was taken by the Pittsburgh Steelers as the second overall selection in the 1945 Draft. Despite having 45 first rounders (the most in SEC history), Florida has never had a player selected No. 1 overall. The most Florida players ever selected by NFL teams in one draft was in 1978 when UF had 10 players selected. Demonstrating that the best teams do not always feature the most picks, that Florida team went 6–4–1. The Pittsburgh Steelers have drafted the most Gators with 24 picks followed by the Chicago Bears with 19, the New York Giants with 17, and the Denver Broncos and San Francisco 49ers with 16 each. A total of 322 Florida players have been taken in the draft.

Emmitt Smith was the first Florida player to declare early, leaving UF after his junior season in 1989. He was selected 17th by the Dallas Cowboys and went on to become the NFL's all-time leading rusher. The most juniors to declare (five) occurred in 2003 after Ron Zook's first season and in 2010 after Florida's two-year run of 26 wins.

Here is a list of some of Florida's most significant players and where they were drafted:

- Steve Spurrier, 1967, third pick, San Francisco 49ers
- Danny Wuerffel, 1997, 99th pick, New Orleans Saints
- Wilber Marshall, 1984, 11th pick, Chicago Bears
- Tim Tebow, 2010, 25th pick, Denver Broncos
- Jack Youngblood, 1971, 20th pick, Los Angeles Rams
- Jimmy DuBose, 1976, 30th pick, Tampa Bay Buccaneers
- Wes Chandler, 1978, third pick, New Orleans Saints
- Carlos Alvarez, 1972, 390th pick, Dallas Cowboys
- Fred Taylor, 1998, ninth pick, Jacksonville Jaguars
- Percy Harvin, 2009, 22nd pick, Minnesota Vikings
- Cris Collinsworth, 1981, 37th pick, Cincinnati Bengals
- Jevon Kearse, 1999, 16th pick, Tennessee Titans

The years following Florida's three national championships saw a total of 16 players drafted, but nine of them were chosen in one draft (the 2007 NFL Draft). Ike Hilliard, Reidel Anthony, Wuerffel, and Jeff Mitchell were chosen in the 1997 NFL Draft.

The 2007 Draft included Jarvis Moss, Reggie Nelson, Ray McDonald, Joe Cohen, Marcus Thomas, Ryan Smith, Dallas Baker, DeShawn Wynn, and Brandon Siler. The 2009 Draft had Percy Harvin, Louis Murphy, and Cornelius Ingram but didn't include Tebow and Brandon Spikes, who decided to return for their senior seasons. They entered the 2010 Draft, which had nine Gators selected, including six in the first two rounds.

# The 2006 Recruiting Class

They didn't all pan out. That never happens in college football. There were players who were busts, and others transferred away from Florida. But when Urban Meyer put together the class that was announced in February of 2006, it changed the UF football program.

That class would help Florida win two national titles, and many of them were still around to have a shot at a third one, which was stopped in the SEC Championship Game by Alabama. During the four years from 2006 to 2009, Florida would win 13 games three times.

Quarterback Tim Tebow was the key. He was already being called "The Chosen One" before he made his announcement about where he would go to school. Tebow was homeschooled by his mother, Pam, and played high school football in Florida at Nease, which is located between Jacksonville and St. Augustine. Tebow, who accounted for 12,960 total yards at Nease, was heavily recruited, and his final decision came down to Florida and Alabama. Alabama coach Mike Shula and the Tebow family developed a special relationship. When the Crimson Tide slammed Florida 31–3 in Tuscaloosa, Alabama, Tebow was at the game, and the Alabama fans were chanting his name in the second half of the game. "It was a good feeling because it made me feel wanted there," Tebow said. "I've had people recognize me before but never like that."

The draw to Florida, though, was powerful. Tebow's parents had met when they were students at UF. Tebow had a poster of Florida quarterback Danny Wuerffel on his wall when he was growing up. Tebow had been to dozens of Florida games. Still it was a tough decision. Meyer was heading into his second season at Florida, and there was some uncertainty whether his spread offense would work in the SEC.

Meyer later told the story about a recruiting trip in Pennsylvania with defensive coordinator Greg Mattison when they discussed landing Tebow. "I had convinced myself that if we lose him, we'll still be okay," Meyer said. "Then Greg Mattison looked at me, and it's about five degrees out. We're sitting there on the plane, and I'm freezing. He said, 'You realize if we don't get Tim, that will set the program back 10 years.' I said, 'Shut up'…I got so upset with him—I grabbed a blanket and didn't talk to him the rest of the trip. He was right."

As a freshman, Tebow was used as a backup to Chris Leak and had a huge impact as Florida won the national title. He was so popular at Florida that fans booed during the Kentucky game when Tebow came out of the game for Leak. Tebow won the Heisman Trophy the next year and a second national title in 2008. But to say this class was all about Tim Tebow would be a tremendous understatement.

Florida also went into Virginia to snag wide receiver Percy Harvin, who would become one of the most dynamic players ever at Florida. "The impact Percy had was tremendous," Meyer said.

The Gators also landed offensive lineman Maurice Hurt and Marcus Gilbert, who would develop into NFL starters. They pulled

Brandon James from St. Augustine High, and he would become a weapon as a kick returner. Mattison had to convince Meyer that James was good enough to play in the SEC. Riley Cooper became a big-time playmaker at wide receiver, and Brandon Spikes was one of the best linebackers to ever play at UF.

The class was ranked No. 1 or No. 2 by most recruiting services, depending on how they felt about Southern Cal's recruits. But the impact that class made was undeniable.

## 64 Sing Florida Songs

On a good day, there is a lot of singing going on at a Florida football game. The alma mater is sung before the game, and "We Are the Boys" is a staple between the third and fourth quarters. When the Gators win, the players join the Florida band for the alma mater and then a rousing edition of the fight song.

The alma mater was written in 1925 by Milton Yeats, who was a member of the University Quartet.

*Florida, our Alma Mater*
*Thy glorious name we praise All thy loyal sons and daughters*
*A joyous song shall raise*
*Where palm and pine are blowing*
*Where southern seas are flowing*
*Shine forth thy noble Gothic walls*
*Thy lovely vineclad halls*
*'Neath the Orange and Blue victorious our love shall never fail*
*There's no other name so glorious*
*All hail, Florida, hail.*

There were plenty of Gator fans who didn't know the fight song lyrics until Urban Meyer became the coach in 2005 and made his players learn the words so they could sing after victories. It was written by Thornton Whitney Allen and George Hamilton.

*Cheer for the Orange and Blue*
*Waving forever pride of old Flor-i-da*
*May she droop never*
*We'll sing a song for the flag today*
*Cheer for the team at play*
*On to the goal we'll fight our way for Flor-i-da.*
*Go Gators!*

"We Are the Boys" was written by Bob Swanson, a player on the 1920 team, and John Icenhour, a student who wrote it for a barbershop group called The Prickly Heat Quartet. The song became popular in Gainesville nightclubs and was finally introduced to games in 1924. Gator fans added the swaying back and forth.

*We are the boys from old Florida F-L-O-R-I-D-A*
*Where the girls are the fairest*
*The boys are the squarest of any old state down our way, hey!*
*We are all strong for old Florida Down where the old Gators play.*
*In all kinds of weather we'll all stick togetherrrrr for*
*F-L-O-R-I-D-A.*

The last lines of the song have become a rallying cry when things become tough for the football teams. With the advent of social media, fans have plenty of ways to criticize players or coaches. That's when they usually hear it. In all kinds of weather, remember?

# 65 The Pouncey Twins

It's not often that a college football coach can go into one home and find three future NFL players. But that was the case when Urban Meyer recruited at the home of Robert and Lisa Webster in Lakeland, Florida. Their twin sons—Mike and Maurkice Pouncey—would eventually become first-round draft choices. Running back Chris Rainey, who was living with the Websters, would also play in the NFL.

Robert Webster came into Lisa's life when she needed help. She was raising two twin boys, and their biological father had left when they were less than a year old. Webster married Lisa, fell in love with her kids, and pushed them toward sports. The Websters also took in Rainey, who came from a broken home with an imprisoned mother.

By the time the Pounceys were helping Lakeland High win a third straight high school title as seniors, schools were breaking down the doors trying to recruit them. The Pounceys originally committed to Florida State, but Meyer was able to convince them to switch to Florida. "I don't think I've ever done that—recruit a pair of identical twins," Meyer said. "It was unique, but what made it unique was how unique they were. They were the greatest practice players I've ever been around."

Mike and Maurkice were actually James and LaShawn on their birth certificates. "We didn't like those names, so we made up Mike and Maurkice," Mike Pouncey said. "Mom finally let us do it, and it has been that way ever since."

The trick for the media was to tell them apart. Meyer said he could always tell who was who because Mike has a mark on his face

## Special Awards

Many Florida football players have won national awards (including three Heisman Trophy winners), but three in-house honors are special to the players.

The Fergie Ferguson Award is given to the player who displays character, leadership, and courage. One of the best all-around athletes to ever attend UF, Forrest "Fergie" Ferguson played both ways from 1939 to 1941 and was the state boxing champion as well as the national AAU javelin champ. He joined the Army when World War II broke out and led a charge at Omaha Beach during D-Day. Wounded during the attack, Ferguson never recovered from the wounds, passing away in 1954.

The first Fergie Ferguson Award was given to fullback Malcolm Hammack in 1954. Some of the other significant winners include:

1958—QB Jimmy Dunn

1966—QB Steve Spurrier

1970—DE Jack Youngblood

1975—FB Jimmy DuBose

1985—RB Neal Anderson

1987—QB Kerwin Bell

2000—QB Jesse Palmer

2007—WR Andre Caldwell

In 1995 linebacker Ben Hanks won the award. Spurrier recruited Hanks, but he was not going to be admitted to school until Spurrier lobbied for him, telling school officials he believed Hanks could complete the class work. Hanks was admitted and became the first player to wear No. 11 when Spurrier unretired his own jersey number.

The James W. Kynes Award is given to the player who exhibits the mental and physical toughness that Kynes showed during his time as a Gator. The captain of the 1949 team, the lineman and two-way player was the last Florida player to play in every minute of a game. Until 2011 the award always went to an offensive lineman. In 2011 it was given to quarterback John Brantley, who fought through injuries throughout his junior and senior years. (He also shared the Ferguson Award in 2011 with linebacker Lerentee McCray.) Guard David Williams received the first Kynes Award in 1986. He won it again in 1988.

Other significant winners include:

1992 and 1995—OG Reggie Green

1996—OG Donnie Young

2000—OT Mike Pearson

2003—OG Shannon Snell

2009—C Maurkice Pouncey

2010—C Mike Pouncey

Voted on by the players, the Ray Graves Award is given to the team MVPs. Graves, the Florida coach from 1960 to 1969, won 70 games during that span. He also coached Florida's first Heisman winner when Spurrier won the award in 1966. Tight end Kirk Kirkpatrick won the first Ray Graves Award in 1990.

Other significant winners include:

1993—RB Errict Rhett

1995 and 1996—QB Danny Wuerffel

1997—RB Fred Taylor

2000—WR Jabar Gaffney

2001 and 2002—QB Rex Grossman

2007, 2008, and 2009—QB Tim Tebow

*(He shared the award with cornerback Joe Haden in '09.)*

2010—SS Ahmad Black

2011—RB Chris Rainey

just below his right eye. Some media members noted that Mike had flames tattooed on his arm, and Maurkice didn't. So as long as they were sleeveless, they could tell the difference.

At Florida, their impact was noticeable and immediate. Maurkice moved into the starting lineup as a true freshman, playing right guard during Tim Tebow's Heisman Trophy season. Mike waited for his chance, but it came on the other side of the ball. Florida was so depleted on the defensive line that Meyer inserted Mike at defensive tackle. "We wanted to redshirt him, but we had no choice," Meyer said. "Maurkice was more advanced as a lineman than Mike, but by the time Mike left, he was just as good."

Maurkice started 11 games in 2007, and Mike had an interception in the 2008 Capital One Bowl against Michigan. In 2008 the brothers were back together and next to each other. Maurkice, wearing No. 56, started all 14 games at center. Mike, wearing No. 55, was the right guard. Together they helped Florida win the 2008 national championship. During the week of the Florida State game late in that 2008 season, Robert Webster lost his right leg when a train ran over it. His sons visited him in the hospital where he told them to go back to school and beat FSU. The Gators did just that, winning the road game 45–15.

In 2009 the Pouncey twins helped Florida win all 12 regular season games before an SEC Championship Game loss to Alabama spoiled the season. After being a big part of 35 wins in three seasons, Maurkice decided to enter the NFL Draft to help the family pay the medical bills that were stacking up.

Mike stayed behind, shifted to center, and waited until after his senior season to turn pro. Both were selected in the first round. Maurkice was drafted by the Pittsburgh Steelers in 2010, and the Miami Dolphins drafted Mike in 2011.

# The Walk-Ons

Recruiting is an inexact science. Not only do football coaches miss on can't-miss prospects, but they miss on players who end up being major players. Florida has a rich tradition of players who walk on to the football team and eventually earn scholarships.

UF has had seven walk-ons who eventually became All-SEC players. Some of those players received "preferred" walk-on status, which means that they were allowed to register for classes ahead of the regular students and receive all of the benefits that scholarship players receive—except the scholarship itself.

Here are the 10 best walk-ons in Florida history:

**1. Kerwin Bell**

Bell had one scholarship offer coming out of high school in tiny Mayo, Florida. But rather than go to Valdosta State, he chose to walk on at Florida because he felt he could play in the SEC. A slew of injuries at the quarterback position pushed Bell into the starting job as a freshman against Miami in Tampa, Florida. He would guide the 1984 Gators to 9–1–1 seasons in both 1984 and 1985. Bell ended his career with 7,585 passing yards and 56 touchdown passes.

**2. Louis Oliver**

Oliver was a hard-hitting safety who combined with Jarvis Williams to give Florida one of the most physical secondaries in the country in 1985. He finished his UF career with 11 interceptions and was the first Florida defensive back to become a two-time All-American. He was named to *The Gainesville Sun*'s Team of the Century in 2006. The Miami Dolphins selected Oliver in the first round of the 1989 NFL Draft.

## 3. Chris Doering

Doering was a skinny wide receiver at P.K. Yonge Developmental Research School in Gainesville and had always dreamed of playing for the Gators, but Florida coach Steve Spurrier didn't offer him a scholarship. Doering went to UF anyway and turned into one of the best receivers in school history with 149 career catches and 2,107 receiving yards. He's most famous for his 28-yard touchdown catch to beat Kentucky. In 1995 he caught three touchdown passes on the same drive against Georgia. (The first two were nullified by penalties.) Doering was one of the few bright spots in Florida's national championship game loss to Nebraska, catching eight passes for 123 yards.

## 4. Lee McGriff

McGriff was another one of those wide receivers who coaches felt was too small to play in the SEC, but he walked on at Florida and turned into a big-play guy for the Gators. He averaged 18.5 yards a catch as a junior and 19.7 as a senior. McGriff's biggest catch was a leaping grab in the end zone against Georgia in 1973. Florida then hit a two-point conversion to win 11–10.

## 5. Preston Kendrick

Kendrick came to Florida on a wrestling scholarship, but some wrestling teammates convinced him to walk on to the football team where his brother, Vince, was a running back. He became a dominant defensive end from 1972 to 1974. He had six sacks against Ole Miss in 1972.

## 6. Judd Davis

Davis is the only placekicker in the UF Athletic Hall of Fame. He won the Lou Groza Award—which goes to the nation's best placekicker—as a senior and made 33-of-38 kicks from inside the 50.

His most memorable game was his four field goals in the muck and rain against Georgia in 1993.

### 7. Bobby Raymond
Another walk-on placekicker, Raymond was one of the most accurate kickers in UF history. He made 17 consecutive field goals in 1984 and made 43-of-49 kicks during his two-year career.

### 8. Jeff Chandler
Chandler became Florida's all-time leading scorer with 368 points. From 1997 to 2001, the kicker made 67 field goals in 80 attempts.

### 9. Allen Trammell
A defensive back who also played wide receiver on offense, Trammell was a big part of Florida's success during the 1965 season. His interception return for a touchdown sealed Florida's come-from-behind win against Florida State that year.

### 10. John James
James' father, Wilbur, played on the 1928 team that went 8–1. John James averaged 40.3 yards per punt for Florida's 1971 team and was inducted into the UF Athletic Hall of Fame. He served as Gator Boosters director before retiring in 2012.

# 67 Go to a Gator Club Meeting

When Charley Pell got the Gator Clubs cranked up around the state in 1979, he dragged his coaching staff with him to get Gator fans fired up. "He told us that if he looked around at any of those meetings and we were talking to each other instead of the fans, we'd be fired," said Lee McGriff, a coach on Pell's first staff.

When Pell took the job at UF, he had not visited the campus and was stunned by how poor the facilities were. But it was more than that. The Gator Nation did not exist yet. Before Pell became the UF coach, there were only a handful of groups around the state who occasionally would meet to talk about Florida football. Mostly it was a collection of fans who always seemed to be bickering about something. Pell knew he had to bring the fan base together and used his experiences at Clemson to come up with the idea for Gator Clubs.

He couldn't have foreseen what they would become. There are more clubs outside the state of Florida than in the state including:

- Triangle Gator Club—Durham, Raleigh, and Chapel Hill, North Carolina
- Windy City Gator Club—Chicago (of course)
- Rocket City Gator Club—Huntsville, Alabama
- Steel Gator Club—Pittsburgh
- Lone Star Gator Club—Round Rock, Texas
- Bluegrass Gator Club—Louisville, Kentucky
- Hula Gator Club—Honolulu

There are clubs in every corner of the United States, from Seattle to Hartford, Connecticut, and from San Diego to Miami. And there are more than 100 Gator Clubs around the world, including those in Hungary, Japan, England, India, Peru, China, and France.

Carly Schwartz is the president of the Gator Club in England. "Watching the games here is great," she said. "Sometimes it is difficult to watch the games due to the time difference. We get anywhere from 20 to 100 fans per game. Several people who come to our viewing parties are just passing through London and join us for the night."

When the clubs became so numerous that each club had a different set of rules or criteria, the Alumni Association took over. The clubs' main objective is to serve as a place to gather, socialize, and watch Gators games together. Especially in the fall, many of the clubs will have speakers come to talk about Gators football. The Emerald Coast Gator Club in Destin, Florida, meets at a restaurant on the water. The Treasure Beach Gator Club meets in a sports bar decorated with Gators memorabilia. The two clubs are seven hours apart but share the same Gulf of Mexico out the window and the same love for the Gators.

The lucky clubs get to hear their head coach speak once a year. Under Pell and into the Steve Spurrier era, the coaches used to speak to as many clubs as possible. But the University Athletic Association felt the coaches were spreading themselves too thin and began to pull back when Ron Zook became the coach. Current coach Will Muschamp spoke to only nine Gator Clubs in 2013, but he sent assistants to four more.

The Gator Clubs do more than serve as a place to get together for cold ones and some sports talk. They help provide scholarships to UF through different fund-raising and offer special programs to UF alumni under 35. Each year the Gator Gala recognizes the best clubs. The Central Florida Gator Club and the Gotham Gator Club in New York City took home the top awards in 2012.

The clubs are open to all alumni, parents, friends, and students of the University of Florida. And if you don't want to travel to visit one, maybe you can start your own. Here is what you need to do according to the UF alumni website:

- Check the list of alumni clubs to be sure there is no chapter in your area. If a club does not exist, contact the Alumni Association to determine if there are the minimum number of alumni and dues-paying members in your area.
- Join the Alumni Association. You (and all future officers) must be a member to organize a club.

- An organizational meeting will occur in your area to inform and assist you in your development plan with the University of Florida Alumni Association (UFAA).
- UFAA will prepare a solicitation letter/email for alumni and friends in your area. After approval of your basic plan, the association will assist you in mailing an initial letter and leadership solicitation to alumni and friends in the area, explaining that a club is in the start-up phase and include directions on how to become a member.

# 68 All in the Family

Florida families stick together. It doesn't always work this way, but usually when a father or brother goes to UF to play football, the next in line follows suit. There are all kinds of brother combinations in UF history, including Vince and Preston Kendrick, Tyson and Glenn Sever, Mike and Maurkice Pouncey. There are father-and-son examples such as Bruce and Brad Culpepper, Ray and Ray McDonald Jr., and Fred Taylor and current UF running back Kelvin Taylor. But here are the five families with multiple Gators players who had the most impact.

### 1. The Gaffneys

Donald was the first African American quarterback to start for Florida when he did so in 1973 at Auburn. He remained the UF quarterback through the 1975 season. His brother, Derrick, was a standout wide receiver for the Gators from 1975 to 1977 and had a long career in the NFL. Another brother, Warren, was starting at defensive back at the same time as Derrick. Johnny, the youngest of the brothers, played briefly at Florida in 1980. The best of the Gaffneys, though, was Derrick's son, Jabar, who caught 27 touchdown passes in 2000 and 2001 and was an All-American wide receiver as a sophomore. He owns the Florida record for most 100-yard receiving games with 15.

## 2. The Jacksons

Willie was the first African American to sign with Florida and had a stellar career as both a wide receiver and a kick returner for the Gators from 1970 to 1972. His son, Willie Jr., was the go-to guy in Florida's offense from 1991 to 1993 and ranks third on UF's all-time receiving list with 162 catches. Another son, Terry, split time with Fred Taylor and Reidel Anthony as the tailbacks of the 1996 national championship season. He also led Florida in rushing in 1998.

## 3. The McGriffs

Perry was the trendsetter when he led the Gators in receiving in 1959. He was actually an even better baseball player, earning All-SEC honors. His cousin, Lee, was one of the best receivers of the 1970s for Florida. Despite playing in an era when Florida didn't throw much, Lee led the SEC in receptions in 1974. Lee's son, Travis, played from 1995 to 1998 and had an explosive senior season when he caught 70 passes for 1,357 yards and 10 touchdowns. Perry's son, Mark, was a tight end at Florida from 1986 to 1988. Mark's son, Ryan, was accepted as a preferred walk-on at Florida in 2011.

## 4. The Brantleys

John came to UF from nearby Ocala, Florida, and won the quarterback job in 1978, throwing for 1,334 yards and 11 touchdowns. He was injured in the second game of the 1979 season and did not return. His brother, Scot, was one of the best linebackers to ever play at Florida. He ranks second all-time in total tackles at UF despite missing almost all of his senior season with a concussion. John's son, John, started at quarterback for Florida in 2010 and 2011. Despite struggling through injuries, he threw for more than 2,000 yards in each of those seasons.

### 5. The Kynes

James Kynes was a two-way player who excelled on both sides of the ball for the Gators from 1946 to 1949. He was Florida's first All-SEC lineman. His son, Jimbo, was the starting center at UF in 1974 when the Gators introduced their wishbone attack. Another son, Billy, was a backup quarterback from 1975 to 1976 and went on to earn a Rhodes scholarship. Billy's son, Matt, was a walk-on quarterback for Urban Meyer's first UF team in 2005.

# 69 All-Americans

Every day that he went to practice, safety Matt Elam looked at them. He would walk up the stairs from the Florida locker room to the entrance of the Heavener Complex and look down at the pavers decorated with the greatest names in Florida history. "That's what I wanted," he said. "I'd look at those names and I wanted to be one of them."

Elam received the honor after his junior season at Florida when he was named a first-team All-American by the Associated Press. That means he will have his own paver on the southwest corner of the football stadium with his name and the year he won the honor. He will be joined by a pair of teammates—defensive tackle Sharrif Floyd and kicker Caleb Sturgis.

Only first-team All-Americans are honored with the granite pavers, which surrounds the large Bull Gator that sits outside the entrance to the UF's coaches offices. They were installed prior to the 2009 football season when the Heavener Complex was built. Long before construction had completed, Florida coach Urban Meyer showed off the 18-inch-by-18-inch granite pavers to reporters. "I got a little emotional the first time I saw it," Meyer said. "Guys gave their life and their soul to make this program great, and now they're permanently part of the history in the greatest stadium in all of college football...out there where everybody can see them and embrace what they've done. We're where we are today because of all the things those guys did in the past and we need to do more to honor them.

Florida has had no shortage of players who have received All-American honors. Here's a look at the 66 other players (besides Floyd, Elam, and Sturgis) worthy of pavers on Florida's version of the Walk of Fame:

1928—**Dale Van Sickel** was a two-way player and a top receiver for a team that scored 336 points in nine games.

1941—**Forrest "Fergie" Ferguson** was ahead of his time as a receiver and set records that wouldn't be broken until Steve Spurrier came along.

1952—**Charlie LaPradd** was a two-way lineman and then an Army paratrooper before resuming his college career.

1956—**John Barrow** was the SEC Linemen of the Year in 1956 who went on to play 14 years in the Canadian Football League.

1958—**Vel Heckman** was an import from Pennsylvania who used his quickness to become a tremendous defensive tackle.

1964—**Larry Dupree** ran for 1,725 yards in his career and was All-SEC three times.

1965—**Lynn Matthews** was a defensive end who specialized in the big play.

1965—**Bruce Bennett** was a member of *The Gainesville Sun's* All-Century team and had 13 career interceptions.

1965—**Larry Gagner** played guard and was one of the best to ever play at Florida before enjoying a long NFL career.

1965—**Charlie Casey** caught 114 passes in three seasons, including 58 as a senior as Steve Spurrier's favorite target.

1965 and 1966—**Steve Spurrier** won the Heisman Trophy and broke every school passing and total offense record.

1966—**Bill Carr** started 32 consecutive games at center and became Florida's athletic director.

1968—**Larry Smith** scored on the last carry of his career against Miami despite a hamstring injury and finished his career with 2,186 yards rushing.

1969—**Carlos Alvarez** made 88 catches as a sophomore to set the school record.

1969— **Steve Tannen** had 11 interceptions as a defensive back and four punt returns for touchdowns during career.

1970—**Jack Youngblood** was named to SEC's Team of Decade in the 1970s before the defensive end entered the NFL Hall of Fame.

1971—**John Reaves** finished his career as the NCAA's all-time leading passer.

1974—**Burton Lawless** started three seasons as a pulling guard.

1974—**Ralph Ortega** had 357 tackles in three seasons and forced 12 fumbles.

1975—**Sammy Green** had 202 tackles during his senior season.

1976 and 1977—**Wes Chandler** was a remarkable receiver who also played some running back at UF.

1980—**Cris Collinsworth** was an excellent wide receiver who also has the longest touchdown pass in NCAA history.

1980—**David Little** was a linebacker and still holds Florida record for most career tackles.

1981—**David Galloway** was one of the most dominant defensive tackles ever at UF.

1982 and 1983—**Wilber Marshall** was a linebacker who might have been the best defensive player ever for the Gators.

1984—**Lomas Brown** was a prototype offensive tackle who started 31 of his last 33 games.

1984 and 1985—**Alonzo Johnson** was a linebacker who had 27 sacks and 55 tackles for a loss in his career.

1985 and 1986—**Jeff Zimmerman** was an offensive guard and part of Florida's Great Wall.

1987—**Clifford Charlton** was an outside linebacker who went on to be a first-round selection of the Cleveland Browns.

1987—**Jarvis Williams** started every game for four straight seasons.

1987 and 1988—**Louis Oliver** was a big-hitting safety who had a nose for the ball.

1988—**Trace Armstrong** transferred from Arizona State, but his lone year at Florida was excellent.

1989—**Emmitt Smith** went on to become the NFL's all-time leading rusher.

1990—**Huey Richardson** ended his career with 26½ sacks and was a first-round pick by the Pittsburgh Steelers.

1990—**Will White** was a safety who had seven interceptions in his senior season.

1991—**Brad Culpepper** was an undersized nose tackle who compensated with his great quickness.

1993—**Errict Rhett** remains Florida's all-time leading rusher.

1993—**Judd Davis** won the Lou Groza Award in 1993 as well.

1994—**Kevin Carter** was a dominant defensive end from Tallahassee.

1994—**Jack Jackson** finished his three-year career with 29 touchdown catches.

1995—**Jason Odom** was a four-year starter at right tackle.

1995 and 1996—**Danny Wuerffel** threw for 10,875 career yards and won the Heisman Trophy.

1996—**Reidel Anthony** was one of Wuerffel's top targets, and the receiver set an SEC record with 18 touchdown catches in a season.

1996—**Ike Hilliard** had 29 touchdowns and 126 catches during UF career.

1997—**Fred Weary** had 15 career interceptions, which set a Florida record.

1997—**Jacquez Green** had 61 catches for 1,024 yards during 1997 season.

1997—**Fred Taylor** was a running back who had eight 100-yard performances during his senior season.

1998—**Mike Peterson** was the heady linebacker and rock of the great 1998 defense.

1998—**Jevon Kearse** was nicknamed "the Freak" and one of those players for which offenses had to gameplan.

1999 and 2000—**Alex Brown** was a defensive end who had more sacks (33) than any other Gators player.

2000—**Lito Sheppard** was a great cover cornerback who also excelled as a punt returner.

2001—**Jabar Gaffney** was almost booted from team but rallied to catch 27 touchdown passes in two seasons.

2001—**Rex Grossman** was a quarterback who made a good case to win the Heisman Trophy that season as well.

2001—**Mike Pearson** was a steady tackle and also twice earned All-SEC honors.

2003—**Keiwan Ratliff** once picked off three passes in a game against Arkansas.

## All-American Stuntman

Many of Florida's All-Americans found success in the NFL, but Florida's first to receive the honor found greater glory in Hollywood. Dale Van Sickel played for the Gators from 1927 to 1929 and coached for a bit after he received his degree. But he eventually wound up getting into the movie business as a stuntman. He appeared in 294 movies (the first was the Marx Brothers' *Duck Soup*) and more than 170 television shows.

Van Sickel became the founding member of the Stuntmen's Association of Motion Pictures and was the organization's first president. He died in 1977 of complications from a stunt car crash.

2003—**Shannon Snell** was a powerful guard who started 33 games.

2006—**Reggie Nelson** was a hard-hitting safety who could cover the whole field.

2007 and 2008—**Percy Harvin** also was the first player in school history to have 100 yards rushing and receiving in a single game.

2007—**Tim Tebow** also was first sophomore to win the Heisman Trophy that year.

2008—**Brandon James** was one of the best punt and kickoff returners in UF history.

2008 and 2009—**Brandon Spikes** was the Tebow for the defense.

2009—**Joe Haden** was a cornerback who started from the first game of his freshman season.

2009—**Aaron Hernandez** likely was the best tight end ever at Florida.

2009—**Maurkice Pouncey** dominated at center after starting at guard.

2010—**Chas Henry** was a Ray Guy Award-winning punter who also took over field goals duties because of an injury.

# 70 The Hiring of Urban Meyer

Jeremy Foley remembers the movie he saw that day. It was *After the Sunset* starring Pierce Brosnan, but he can't tell you anything about it. It was December 2, 2004, and he had just offered the vacant Florida head coaching job to Utah coach Urban Meyer.

But while Foley, the Florida athletic director, and his associate AD Greg McGarity watched the movie in Salt Lake City, Utah, Notre Dame was at the Meyer house, making a pitch to lure him to succeed Ty Willingham.

Questions swirled in Foley's head. Meyer had called Notre Dame his dream job. Were the Gators going to finish second? Was it time to call Foley's second choice—Louisville head coach Bobby Petrino? And if he turns me down, then what? There was no third option at the time.

From the firing of Ron Zook on October 25 to this point in time, Foley and his staff had made an exhaustive search to find the next coach at UF. They compiled notebooks thick with information on the possibilities, but Foley had pledged to Florida president Bernie Machen he would not talk to anyone until after their regular seasons had completed. By the time the staff finished, they had 15 coaches considered legitimate candidates.

Foley took another swing at Oklahoma coach Bob Stoops to gauge his interest but found out that the answer was the same as it was in 2002 when Steve Spurrier resigned. Iowa coach Kirk Ferentz wasn't interested. Cleveland Browns coach Butch Davis showed some interest but changed his mind. After the Browns fired Davis, Foley made another call to Davis' representative, but the coach still wasn't interested. Media and fans assumed Meyer would be the top choice because Machen had been the president at Utah before coming to Florida, and Meyer was the hot coach, having guided the Utes to an undefeated season.

Foley flew to a home he owns in Stowe, Vermont, the day before Thanksgiving and then to Salt Lake City the following day. He had set up a meeting with Meyer and his wife, Shelley. Both Foley and Meyer had plenty of questions. At one point Meyer excused himself to do a phone interview with ABC during the Texas–Texas A&M game. "You could have really caused a stir if

*Florida athletic director Jeremy Foley (right) introduces new coach Urban Meyer to the media on December 7, 2004.* (AP Images)

you told them who was sitting in your living room," Foley said to Meyer after the interview.

When Foley returned to Gainesville, he told Machen that Meyer was the guy he wanted to hire. "He's pretty impressive, isn't he?" Machen said to Foley.

But then Willingham was fired. Foley called Meyer, who told him of Notre Dame's interest. Foley enlisted Christine Donovan, the wife of Florida's basketball coach Billy Donovan, to help recruit Shelley. The day after Florida offered Meyer the job and Notre Dame made its pitch, Foley returned to the Meyer house. Meyer said to him, "I'm close to walking across this room and shaking your hand."

There were still some details to work out, including an up-front bonus to help the Meyers purchase a home in Gainesville. Meyer wanted to hold the announcement because his Utah team was about to be named as one of the teams playing in the Fiesta Bowl. They decided to wait until after that announcement on Sunday. But when Foley was heading back to his hotel, he saw 26 messages on his cell phone. The story was breaking. He drove back to Meyer's house and told him, "We're going to have to do this sooner than later."

Florida announced the hiring the next day. Meyer coached his team to a win in the Fiesta Bowl and then hopped on a chartered plane with Foley to Gainesville. He had been there before. When he was recruiting the state of Florida as a Notre Dame assistant, Meyer stopped in Gainesville to look at the stadium. Now he was going to coach in it.

At his introductory press conference, Meyer won the room. He talked about embracing the past and how he was a fan of Spurrier's teams in the 1990s—exactly what Florida fans wanted to hear.

# 71

## Go to Fan Day

On a Saturday in the middle of August when the air is sticky and the love bugs are loving, you can't wait for the season to get here. You have started counting the days. That's why Fan Day is so popular. Florida fans can chat with some of their favorite players there and get to know some of the newbies.

As an autograph session, however, it leaves a little to be desired. Fans at most schools can bring footballs, pictures, hats, etc. to be signed by the players and coaches from their favorite teams. Not at Florida.

In 2000 the University Athletic Association decided that fans bringing memorabilia in to be signed could expose the football program to possible NCAA violations. The concern was that a dealer could have a couple of footballs signed by—say, Rex Grossman and Jabar Gaffney—and then sell them for hundreds of dollars.

Two issues factored into the autograph restriction decision. People would violate the "two items per person" rule and show up with dozens of footballs in a duffel bag to be signed. Florida tried to police this, but with 100 or so players and coaches, it became difficult. Steve Spurrier also demanded that he and his assistant coaches receive a nominal sum for signing. Spurrier contended that other people were making money off his signature.

At any rate while it's standard policy at many other schools to allow fans to bring stuff from home to be signed (Alabama, for example), Florida fans line up for Fan Day and are given a poster issued by the UAA. That poster—and only that poster—is allowed to be presented for signature. Florida still polices the situation, and there are fans who definitely try to slide in other items. This puts players in the awkward position of having to say no.

Even with the restrictions, Fan Day is a big part of the Gator experience. In addition to the posters each fan receives, they get some face time with the players on the upcoming Gators team, who are seated at a long row of tables. Thousands attend, and fans come from far away and even camp out, waiting for the doors to open. The event is held every year in the O'Connell Center, and starting in 2011 it was combined with the Fan Day for women's volleyball, which has a preseason scrimmage during Fan Day, so the fans can get a double dose of the Gators.

The event is the one chance many of the fans have to interact with players because practices are closed, and the fans who try to get autographs after practices are often shooed away by security personnel.

# 72 Attend Gator FanFest

It started during the 2007 football season as an idea to unite Florida fans in one place rather than wait until the game started. It has become a huge party, an orange-and-blue sea waiting to spill into The Swamp.

Gator FanFest is so big it often doesn't shut down until well after the game starts. "It has really grown," said Mike Hill, Florida's associate athletic director for internal affairs. "It was pretty thin at the beginning. People either didn't know about it or weren't sure about it. They had their own routines at games."

Which is why Florida started the party.

Tailgating tends to spread out the crowd all over the Florida campus and into the nearby neighborhoods. The University Athletic Association wanted a place where Gators fans could mingle. The area that was set aside is a grass lot that rests between the O'Connell Center, where the Gators play basketball and other sports, and the southwestern entrance of the stadium at Gate 2.

FanFest starts three hours before home games, and the centerpiece is the Florida pregame radio show conducted by Steve Russell. The show is broadcast on the university-owned WRUF radio station and the other stations that make up the Gator Radio Network. Former players such as Noah Brindise, Travis McGriff, and James Jones have joined Russell in the past. For a couple of years, CBS Sports Network did a pregame television show from different campuses and made several visits to FanFest.

Kids can have their faces painted at FanFest and win prizes, depending on that day's sponsor. There are anywhere between 25 to 40 vendors set up in the area. "Some sponsors really blow it out when they are there," Hill said.

The UAA has set up televisions and chairs, giving fans the option of either watching a game that is going on or playing college football on an Xbox. The other Gator teams make an appearance at each FanFest, serving as another major attraction. It might be the UF softball team, the gymnastics team, or the basketball team mingling with the crowd and signing autographs.

The action tends to wind down as the start of the game nears, but Florida fans have been notoriously late arrivals, especially for non-conference games that are not Florida State, and FanFest keeps the music blaring well after kickoff. Some fans even come to the party without any intention of going to the game.

FanFest also makes scaled-down appearances on the road for big games. And for bowl games, FanFest is out in full force usually the day before the game with cheerleaders and the Pride of the Sunshine—the University of Florida Marching Gator Band.

# 0–10–1

To some Gator fans, it serves as a badge of honor. You can't really be a Gators fan unless you endured 0–10–1. If as many people were in the stands who now claim to be, Florida Field would have been standing room only.

The 1979 season was the most futile and yet one of the most famous in Florida history. It was the last time Florida has had a losing season—and, boy, did the Gators lose. It was a season brimming with optimism because Florida had a new coach, Charley Pell, and he had won at Clemson. Doug Dickey had been shown the door, and the thinking was that Pell could put the Gators back on track.

But festering below the surface of the football program was a problem. "Charley spent the whole spring out raising money and friends for the program," said UF historian Norm Carlson. "He had a major drug problem going on and he wasn't here to have his finger on the pulse of it. When he did get back, it was too late."

In his later years before he passed away, Pell was asked about the 1979 season and said, "That was the year I got involved with the DEA."

He told the story of the night before a game when a player called to complain that his roommate was smoking marijuana in the next bed, and the smoke was making it impossible for him to sleep. A trainer was sent to confiscate the drugs. On the following Monday, the player showed up at Pell's office demanding his weed. "That's what I was dealing with," Pell said.

Florida's 1979 team, though, still had Cris Collinsworth at wide receiver and John Brantley at quarterback and his All-American brother, Scot Brantley, at middle linebacker. Surely there would be enough talent to win. "I came in, thinking that by myself," Collinsworth said, "I could win one game."

Florida lost a tough opener against Houston before coming home for the high point of the season: a tie.

The Gators had a chance to win that game against Georgia Tech on a field goal by Brian Clark, but Lawrence Lowe leapt over the pile of bodies to block the kick on the last play of the game. It was not a good night for the Gators. Earlier in the game, Scot Brantley suffered a concussion and would not play the remainder of the year. And his brother, John, suffered a knee injury in an unlikely way.

At the end of the third quarter, Gators fans would heave the lids from their sodas onto the field, making it rain plastic. But John Brantley rolled out early in the fourth quarter, stepped on one of those lids, and blew out his knee. "So there we are—Scot and I— sitting in beds next to each other in the infirmary while the game is being played," John Brantley said. "That was a sick feeling."

Florida tried everything to replace Brantley at quarterback. They used Larry Ochab, who earned the nickname "Dr. O" because he was short and stocky and looked more like the pre-med student he was than an athlete. They moved Johnell Brown from running back, Tim Groves from defensive back, and Tyrone Young from wide receiver.

A week after the tie game, Florida led Mississippi State in the fourth quarter but lost. Then they gave up 14 fourth-quarter points to LSU and lost 20–6. There were blowouts (a 40–0 loss to eventual national champion Alabama) and close losses (19–13 to 20th-ranked Auburn), but they were all losses the rest of the way before finally it was over.

The Gators had gone winless.

Collinsworth had spent the year seeing more reporters than passes come his way. He became an unofficial spokesman for the team and later said that all of the interviews he did probably helped him become a polished broadcaster.

Pell knew he had a mess on his hands. Not only had he just led an 0–10–1 season, but he also had accepted the job without setting foot on campus. He had no idea how poor the facilities were. Pell raised money to pay for improved facilities and—talent. "He panicked," Carlson said. "He went out and got a bunch of guys and started paying players."

The Gators made the greatest turnaround in NCAA history at the time when they went 8–4 in 1980. But three games into the 1984 season, Pell had been caught by the NCAA and was fired.

# 74 Experience Gator Growl and Homecoming

It started as a simple pep rally, something to encourage the football team for the following day's game. It has turned into a stadium of Florida fans watching light shows, fireworks, and A-list comedians.

Gator Growl is the culmination of the Friday night of homecoming each year at UF. Homecoming began at Florida in 1916, and there was an informal pep rally the night before each game. That pep rally became "Dad's Day" at the all-male school in 1923. The band would play, and the cheerleaders would cheer in anticipation of the game. In 1931 a group of school officials decided the pep rally needed a new name, and "Gator Growl" was born.

As technology improved—so did Growl. The performance has been called the "world's largest student-run pep rally" and includes skits and cameo appearances of celebrities calling out to "let the Gator Growl." In 1976 Growl made entertainers part of its show. Legendary Bob Hope was the first to perform and ended up doing Growl three times. During one appearance he was taping for a television special and stopped his act because the crowd wasn't laughing hard enough. He went backstage and started all over again. Jerry Seinfeld, Bill Cosby (twice), Rodney Dangerfield, Billy Crystal, and Jay Leno are among the big acts who have played Growl. Robin Williams performed in 1982 but set off controversy with his raunchy material. As a result Florida brought back Hope the following year.

The Growl had occasional music acts, but the organizers from Florida Blue Key, a student honor and service society, decided to amp things up in 2007 because of dwindling attendance. Lynyrd Skynyrd showed up, and musical acts have performed every year since. Growl isn't the only activity associated with homecoming, but it is the most famous. Many schools around the country have copied the format.

There is also a race the morning of Gator Growl, a two-mile run down University Avenue called the Gator Gallop. After the race the annual homecoming parade follows the same route going east on University with close to 100,000 people watching from the sidewalks. Heading into its 90th year, the parade is a family-friendly event. It includes floats from area businesses and UF fraternities and sororities, marching bands from all over the area, and politicians riding in vintage cars. Before each homecoming game, Florida Blue Key also hosts an alumni barbecue.

# 75 Alabama: A Familiar Foe

It must have felt strange for Alabama fans at the 2012 SEC Championship Game. Where was Florida?

The Crimson Tide had played in seven previous SEC title games, and each time its opponent was UF. The two schools have combined for 18 appearances in the game since it was created in 1992. The rest of the league has combined for 24. Florida and Alabama have played more times in the title game than they have in the regular season during the last 20 years. The two teams, appropriately enough, played in the original game in '92.

Here's a look at the history of Florida vs. Alabama in the SEC title game.

**1992**: Antonio Langham's interception return for a score gave Alabama a 28–21 victory. When the idea of a conference championship game was first announced, critics said the SEC would never win another national title because it was adding an extra game. Alabama won it all this year, and the league has won 11 national crowns since the SEC Championship Game was born.

**MVP**: Langham

**1993:** In the second and final game played at Birmingham's Iron Bowl, Shayne Edge made a key first-down run on a fake punt, and Terry Dean lit up the Alabama defense for a 28–13 win. Florida went on to win the Sugar Bowl in New Orleans.

**MVP:** Dean

**1994:** Steve Spurrier had to resort to trickery for the winning touchdown drive in a 24–23 victory against the undefeated Tide. He had Danny Wuerffel fake an injury and put Eric Kresser in the game. Kresser then launched a 25-yard pass to Ike Hilliard. With Wuerffel back in, Florida ran a flea flicker with receiver Chris Doering throwing to Aubrey Hill to the 2-yard line. Wuerffel then hit Doering for the game-winner.

**MVP:** Defensive tackle Ellis Johnson

**1996:** In a shootout in the Georgia Dome, Wuerffel's 85-yard touchdown pass to Jacquez Green was the clincher. Alabama had

## The Other Three

It was a few hours before the 2006 SEC Championship Game, and Urban Meyer was a wreck. His former boss and close friend, Earle Bruce, sat next to him in the hotel lobby. He asked Meyer how he was doing. "Not good," Meyer said.

Bruce then gave Meyer a good talking to about how the Gators had made it to Atlanta by not playing with fear. "You got here with gimmicks and trick plays," Bruce said. "Don't forget that." Meyer wrote it on his sheet, and sure enough, a fake punt turned the game around, and a wide receiver pass to a tight end clinched Florida's 38–28 win against Arkansas.

It was one of three games that Florida has played in Atlanta that did not involve Alabama. The Gators also beat Arkansas in 1995 on their way to the national title game. Florida won 34–3 but led only 24–3 before Ben Hanks intercepted a lateral and returned it 95 yards for a touchdown.

The Gators' other SEC Championship Game victory came against Auburn in 2000. Rex Grossman threw four touchdown passes—three of them in the first 22 minutes of the game—as Florida won 28–6 in a rematch of a regular season game.

drawn to within 31–28 before the play late in the third quarter. Florida would go on to win its first national championship.

**MVP:** Wuerffel

**1999:** In a rematch of a game earlier in the season, Alabama blew out Florida 34–7. UF starting quarterback Doug Johnson could not go because of shoulder tendinitis, and Jesse Palmer was the surprise starter. Johnson took a cortisone shot at halftime and started the second half, but his passes bounced into the turf, and Palmer finished the game.

**MVP:** Alabama wide receiver Freddie Milons

**2008:** Tim Tebow had never led Florida to a come-from-behind victory. He checked that off his to-do list when he rallied

Florida to a 31–20 win with 14 fourth-quarter points. Tebow threw for three short touchdown passes in the game, and Florida went on to win the national title.

**MVP:** Tebow

**2009:** It was Alabama's turn to win the big game and end Florida's dream season. The unbeaten Gators lost 32–13 but had a chance late before Tebow threw an interception in the end zone. That caused Urban Meyer to throw his headset, and Alabama fans rejoiced when the video boards later showed Tebow weeping.

**MVP:** Alabama quarterback Greg McElroy

# 76 Tailgators

When you are annually named one of the top party schools in the nation, the party can start at any time. That's why on gamedays you can see people starting to tailgate near campus in the wee hours of the morning—and that's for night games.

Tailgating is part of the social fabric of Gainesville and an opportunity to get together with friends to eat, drink, and be merry while waiting for the Gators to play. And this is not a lonely sport. Most UF fans have a plan that includes finding several parking spots, circling the cars, and laying out a spread. Each partygoer has an assignment for something to bring.

The biggest boosters at UF take it to another level. Not only do they get the best spots, they often have their food either catered or cooked on site. Parking spots for boosters are assigned on a points basis, and those points are determined by the amount of

## Best Tailgating Spots

If you are not a big-time booster with a parking pass near the stadium, you can still set up camp at several prime spots. For $450 fans can get a season pass to the large parking lot behind St. Augustine Church and just a couple of blocks from campus. Mike Martin of Melrose, Florida, and his friends have three spots in the back corner of the lot. "It sets up perfectly for us," Martin said, "because we have a grassy area there, and it's near the bathroom."

Another popular spot is at J.J. Finley Elementary School, which is six blocks from the stadium. The school has a grass field the size of two football fields where fans can also buy annual passes. The Reitz Union is another popular area to park because it has shade in parts of the tailgate areas. Those who arrive at the stadium area very early usually can find spots on campus, and homeowners near the stadium will let you park in their yards for anywhere from $10 to $30. The city now charges those homeowners $52.50 a year for a permit to allow parking during the season.

the contribution. The boosters guaranteed parking spaces are Bull Gators, Grand Gators, Scholarship Club members, Scholarship Partner members, and the grandfathered Fighting Gators.

The north end zone and the O'Connell Center parking lot—both a stone's throw away from the stadium—are the prime locations for the biggest boosters. The north end zone was used for media parking until 2011 when it was re-assigned to boosters with RVs. The media now parks along Stadium Drive near the baseball field.

On gameday the area near the stadium looks like a mall on Black Friday. It seems as if people are constantly making their way from one party to another, often rolling coolers behind them or riding on motorized coolers. Is this a great country or what?

But there are restrictions for tailgating in Gainesville and they can be found on the University Athletic Association's website, Gatorzone.com. The rules include:

- Always practice positive, fan-friendly behavior. Be respectful of those around you and your tailgating area. Remember: drunkenness, obscene, or harassing behavior, and violence or threats of violence will not be tolerated.
- Keep your tailgating area clean and free of litter. "Put it in the can, Gators fan."
- Open containers of alcohol on public streets, sidewalks, and thoroughfares is a violation of City of Gainesville ordinance 4-4B and can result in arrest and/or referral to Student Judicial Affairs.

One thing about tailgating at UF is that it is spread throughout the campus and the area surrounding the campus. You could take a long walk on gameday and see "tailgators" for miles. Their menus will vary, but barbecue is the most popular entree. Cajun food is a must when LSU is in town, and fish tacos are also popular and easy to make.

But for the most part at this party, food is a big deal, but it's still secondary to libations. And the more elaborate tailgates include a generator for electricity and a big-screen television to keep track of the other games.

Tailgating continues to evolve at UF games. Back in the 1950s, fans could bring booze and coolers into the games. And through the 1990s, fans could leave at halftime, go back to their tailgates, and fire them up again. But the SEC prohibited that in 2000. Although there are several prime spots for tailgating, some fans prefer to use the park-and-ride system. There are five locations around town where fans can park and take a shuttle to the stadium.

# 77 Teams of the Century

There were a lot of lists and a lot of honors flying around during the 2006 football season. It was officially recognized as the 100th year of Florida's football program, and the university did everything from hold a gala to unveil the Ring of Honor.

There were also dueling All-Century teams. The University Athletic Association had one where fans could vote on its website. *The Gainesville Sun* had another with fans voting, but the staff at *The Sun* organized the team. By "organize" the newspaper meant it would take the fan votes and mold a team around it.

There were a lot of differences between the two teams, including 13 players on the 24-man *Sun* team who were not on the 26-man Gatorzone.com team. The players on both teams were: quarterback Danny Wuerffel, running back Emmitt Smith, wide receiver Carlos Alvarez, offensive lineman Lomas Brown, center Jeff Mitchell, defensive end Kevin Carter, defensive end Jack Youngblood, defensive tackle Brad Culpepper, linebacker Scot Brantley, linebacker Wilber Marshall, and defensive back Louis Oliver.

But that was in 2006. Since then Florida won two national championships and two SEC titles. Beginning with the 2006 season, Florida had a stretch where they went 48–6. Oh yeah, and they had some guy named Tim Tebow.

A vote taken today might be too soon because the memories are still fresh. But it might look like this:

## Quarterback

Sorry, Danny, you were amazing, but what Tebow did at Florida was ridiculous. He was part of two national titles, won the Heisman

*Wide receiver Percy Harvin, who would make any list of all-time Gators, snares a pass during Florida's 59–20 home victory against Tennessee in 2007.*
(AP Images)

Trophy as a sophomore, and should have won as a junior. And let's face it—he is the most well known UF player ever.

## Running Backs

*The Sun* had Emmitt and Neal Anderson, so we'll stick with it. Yes, Errict Rhett had numbers and is the school's all-time leading rusher, but he'd be third on this list.

## Wide Receivers

So many to choose from, but how do you keep Percy Harvin off this list? He was a faster version of one of the greats—Wes Chandler. Alvarez made our original list, but doesn't Ike Hilliard belong? We'll have to go with a three-receiver set of Harvin, Chandler, and Hilliard.

## Tight end

Florida's tight end history was filled with a lot of strong contenders but no overwhelming player in 2006. It has one now. Aaron Hernandez redefined the position at UF from 2007 to 2009.

## Offensive Line

Brown is a no-brainer. You had to see Burton Lawless play in the early 1970s to understand how good he was. Jason Odom was a rock for four years at tackle under Steve Spurrier. David Williams was a star. The only guy who gets knocked off the original *Sun* list is Jeff Mitchell, and that's because of Maurkice Pouncey's dominance at center.

## Defensive Line

We're going to put Jevon Kearse at end, even though he was a hybrid end-linebacker. And Youngblood is a lock at the other end. Ellis Johnson may have been the best tackle to ever play at Florida.

And we're going to put another end in there by going with Carter. Hey, this All-Century team will be able to rush the passer.

## Linebackers

Even newcomers like Brandon Spikes cannot beat out the trio of Scot Brantley, the late David Little, and Marshall.

## Defensive Backs

Oliver is definitely the strong safety, but we're switching up here and putting Reggie Nelson at free safety. Have you ever seen a guy cover more ground or make more big plays? The corners stay the same—Lito Sheppard and Steve Tannen.

## Specialists

Judd Davis had a great career at UF, but his protégé, Caleb Sturgis, beats him out at placekicker. Bobby Joe Greene is the punter, and we're adding Brandon James as kick returner.

There will be no plaques and no halftime recognition for this new all-time team. And there are so many greats left out. You could put together a second team that some might argue was better than the first team. For example, a backfield of Wuerffel, Rhett, and Fred Taylor would be scary. How about a defensive line of Trace Armstrong, Alex Brown, Sharrif Floyd, and Jarvis Moss?

But as we know from generating a list of chapters for *100 Things Every Florida Fan Should Know & Do Before They Die*, that's the way it is with these lists. Half of the purpose is to generate discussion.

# 78 Load Up on Gators Gear

Many fans used to hit the Gator Shop on the corner of University Avenue and NW 17ᵗʰ St. to make that once-a-year stop to get a hat or shirt for the upcoming season. But after 28 years, increasing rent forced the Gator Shop to close in the summer of 2012. And while there are still several stores (including Gator Mania in the Oaks Mall) that sell Gators gear, the most popular stores are located right in the stadium.

The Gator Locker Room, which is just outside the northeast entrance to The Swamp, is open weekdays from 10 AM to 6 PM and on gamedays. The other Gator Locker Room store in the stadium—located on the south end—is only open on gamedays. The two stores had a combined gross income in 2012 of $2.3 million. Florida pulled in more than $5 million in gross sales from all of its licensing deals in 2012.

The Gator Locker Room is so full of Gators items that it sometimes can be tough to walk around in it. On the average day, only one cash register is open. On a gameday there are nine working cash registers, all humming along with precision. A carload of fans can make a day of the shopping expedition because several bars and restaurants are located right across the street. The old Gator Shop a block east is now a bar called Fat Daddy's. The old Purple Porpoise is now called Gator City but has the same basic premise as the old Porpoise: cheap drinks, pool tables, and televisions. What's not to like?

As soon as you walk into the Gator Locker Room, the game-worn Gators helmets jump out at you. They sell for a mere $399 each. Dozens of footballs are there for purchase just waiting for an autograph. Throughout the store you can find all kinds of shirts, sweatshirts, hats, and jackets with the Gators logo. Need a cutting board for the kitchen? *Got it.* How about a new toaster with the Gators logo? *Yes indeed.* Gators toilet paper? *Sure.* Salt and pepper shakers shaped like Gators helmets? *Check.* Snuggie? *Why not?*

Jerseys are for sale, but if you want a No. 15 jersey in honor of Tim Tebow, you'd better hope there's a straggler remaining. Gators jerseys with that number are no longer being ordered. Jersey numbers have been a pet peeve of the compliance people at the University Athletic Association. It started after Danny Wuerffel's senior season when No. 7 jerseys flew off the shelves.

Concerned that the athletic department could be seen as exploiting Wuerffel or that signed jerseys could end up being sold for profit, Florida decided to offer only one jersey number in 1997—the number 97, and each successive year featured the corresponding number. But in 2002 UF decided to make an exception as part of its enticement to convince Rex Grossman—the Heisman Trophy runner-up in 2001—to stay in school for another year and play for new coach Ron Zook. So the No. 8 jersey was for sale. After Tebow won the Heisman in 2007, UF again decided to make an exception and sell his numbered jersey.

# 79 The Logo Change

One of the most well-known symbols in all of college athletics is only a teenager. The Gators head that is Florida's brand is a relative newbie for college sports fans. But when you see it now, you immediately think of the University of Florida. Whether it's on *SportsCenter* or CBS or the hat you're wearing, Florida's logo stands out against the rest.

But it was not until 1998 that the Gator head became the official logo of Gator sports. In the 1960s the logo was a simple block "F," which was the same as the one on the sides of the Gators helmets. That changed in 1979 when Florida went to a new design. This logo was an elaborate child of the generation, a modern "U" and "F" with a snapping alligator next to the "U" and a graphic of the state of Florida next to the "F." And until 1991 that was the official symbol of the Gators. In 1992 a standing alligator wearing a hat became the official symbol. It was on Gators-related hats and flags, and anything else you can purchase.

But the folks at the University Athletic Association wanted something different. For one thing they had an in-house joke about the feet on the alligator, referring to the symbol as the "chicken-footed Gator." The logo had feet that did look more like a chicken's than an alligator's. "The biggest problem we had was that there was no consistency," said Mike Hill, UF's associate athletic director for internal affairs. "Some people were using the old one. Some were using the alligator. Different teams were using different ones. So we wanted one logo that would say, 'this is the Florida Gators.'"

They went with a simple, yet striking design from a firm in New York. With 20 sharp teeth snarling and its upper lip pointed to the sky, the alligator head in the logo looks menacing. The eye glares angrily—like someone just tried to complete a pass on the Florida secondary. The alligator head is surrounded by an orange-and-blue background that follows the outline of the head where the alligator's eyes are located.

At first some objected to the new logo because the old alligator was synonymous with success for the Florida football team, but acceptance didn't take long. You can still see Florida fans at games wearing gear with the "chicken-footed Gator." But whether at The Swamp or at a family dinner, the 15-year old logo is the dominant way of showing off the team for which you root.

In 2012 Florida decided that the block "F" logo at the center of Florida Field would be replaced. The "F" had been placed there in 1988 as a way of honoring all Gators letterwinners and at the center of a new artificial turf when Florida became the first school to use tufted All-Pro turf. But a 60-foot wide Gator head logo took its place in 2012, and the "F" logos were moved to each 25-yard line. "We didn't get one complaint," Hill said. "Fans like seeing that logo in the middle of the field."

# 80 Gainesville Gators

You would think that any kid who grows up in the Gainesville area would be so overwhelmed by everything Florida Gators that he automatically would enroll at Florida. But it doesn't always work that way.

Florida has lost out on players such as F.W. Buchholz High's Lamar Thomas (Miami), Gainesville High's Clinton Portis (Miami), and P.K. Yonge Developmental Research School's Robert Baker (Auburn). Still the history of Gators football is rich with players who hail from Gainesville.

Here is a list of the best from the Gainesville area:

## 1. Chris Doering
Doering had an amazing career after graduating from P.K. Yonge. The gangly Doering was a huge Gators fan all his life and a big Cris Collinsworth fan, but he ended up with even better numbers than Collinsworth. Doering finished his UF career with 149 catches for 2,107 yards and 31 touchdowns, the most receiving scores in UF history.

## 2. Mike Peterson

Peterson played at Santa Fe High in Alachua, and the former quarterback turned into one of the most steady defenders in UF history. He finished his career with 249 tackles and 8.5 sacks and was an All-American in his senior year (1998). "I tell the young guys all the time—they have to go some [lengths] to be as good as that '98 defense," Peterson said. That defense held UF opponents to one touchdown or fewer in eight games.

## 3. Ricky Nattiel

The Rocket grew up in Archer and attended Newberry High. Nattiel had 2,086 receiving yards for his career and a knack for big plays, including the 96-yard touchdown pass against Georgia in 1984 and the touchdown that allowed Florida to go for two against Auburn in an 18–17 win in 1986. And he was an excellent punt returner.

## 4. Bernie Parrish

A P.K. Yonge alum and former walk-on who would become a two-way player, Parrish excelled as a halfback and cornerback. He received National Player of the Week honors when Florida beat Vanderbilt in 1957, rushing for 111 yards and picking off a pair of passes.

## 5. Doug Johnson

Johnson played minor league baseball after his career at Buchholz and for the most part was the Florida starting quarterback from 1997 to 1999. He finished his career with 7,114 passing yards and 62 touchdown passes.

## 6. Willie Jackson Jr.

Jackson, who went to school at P.K. Yonge, was the first big-time receiver in the Steve Spurrier era. He finished his career with 2,172 yards and had eight 100-yard receiving games during his career from 1990 to 1993.

## 7. Wayne Fields

A standout defensive back at Gainesville High, Fields was a lockdown cornerback for the Gators from 1972 to 1975. His most memorable play was an interception return for a touchdown that clinched a win against Miami during his sophomore year.

## 8. Travis McGriff

McGriff, another P.K. Yonge kid, was a steady wide receiver before exploding in 1998 as a senior. His 70 catches are sixth all time for a season at UF, and his 1,357 yards are an SEC record. McGriff had eight 100-yard games in '98. McGriff's father, Lee, was an All-SEC wide receiver.

## 9. Ian Scott

Scott was a heralded recruit out of Gainesville High who became a standout defensive tackle from 2000 to 2002, plugging holes in the middle and using his quickness to excel. Scott is the only member of this list to jump to the NFL after his junior season. (Parrish left for a baseball career, but he entered the NFL two seasons later and had a great pro career.)

## 10. (tie) Terry Jackson and Doug Dickey

Dickey belongs on this list as a player. The P.K. Yonge product is a member of the Florida-Georgia Hall of Fame as a quarterback. But Jackson, another P.K. Yonge grad and Willie's younger brother, belongs on this list for no other reason than his clinching touchdown run when UF won its first national title. So we'll call it a tie.

# 81 Visit the Heavener Complex

Still getting used to the new environs, head coach Urban Meyer had one simple query. "Where's the front door to this place?" Good question. Although Ben Hill Griffin Stadium houses the football offices, getting inside is almost a like the opening of the old show *Get Smart*.

Although some consider that show timeless, what Meyer wanted—and what Jeremy Foley and his staff had been talking about before Meyer's arrival at UF—was a serious upgrade. The revamped facility would represent a showcase.

The construction began in 2007, and the Bill Heavener Football Complex opened in August of 2008. Heavener, a longtime booster from Winter Park, Florida, and the CEO of Full Sail Real World Education, was the main donor. (He gave $7 million for the naming rights.) But 15 others gave a minimum of $1 million. As a result the $28 million project was privately funded.

Some of the areas built or refurbished during the project are rarely seen by Gators fans. The weight room doubled in size, and the coaches' offices were expanded and modernized. The Gator Room, which the football and other UF athletic teams use for meals and meetings, is also off-limits to the public.

But there is plenty to see. How about a walking tour?

Before you walk up the stairs and into what is basically a Gators football museum, you walk past a 15-foot bronze alligator, a tribute to the 2006 national champions. The donors who paid to provide that photogenic statue are listed on the sides. Each step represents history as there are 18-inch-by-18-inch granite pavers on the ground with each one having the name and year of a Gators All-America player.

Along the low wall to the left are plaques for each member of the NCAA College Football Hall of Fame. As you walk up the stairs, you will see the Tim Tebow Promise from 2008 attached to the wall. Once inside you will first notice the three trophy cases, each containing a crystal ball representing the national champions. Behind each crystal is a constantly changing graphic, depicting scenes from each season.

Three more trophy cases are on the right, and each contains a Heisman Trophy and a bio of the three winners. Florida's SEC championship trophies are displayed in the middle of the room. And to the right and left are individual honors and trophies won by players such as Judd Davis, Lawrence Wright, and Brad Culpepper.

There are several touch-screen televisions where you can choose which rivalry game or SEC championship to watch. And on the high walls to the right are banners honoring championship teams, including those who won BCS bowl games. All in all, it's orange-and-blue heaven for anyone wanting to relive the greatest moments in Gators history.

And to the left, the silver staircase leads to the coaches' offices. Don't even think about going up there. The glass doors can only be opened by a switch inside.

# 82 Travel to an SEC Road Game

The relative no-show at the 2013 Sugar Bowl notwithstanding, Gator Nation tends to be everywhere. Even as the economic issues of the times have made disposable income tighten up, it's not unusual to see Florida fans fill up an entire section of an SEC stadium. For many of those Gators fans, it's not only a chance to support the team, but also a chance to see a different city and stadium.

Nothing is easy for Gators fans. Of the 13 potential road games, 10 of them are more than 500 miles from Gainesville. But any Gators fan, who has been to a stadium when it empties out in the fourth quarter and all that's left is orange and blue, will tell you it's worth it. The usual split for tickets to a road game is 90–10, meaning that 10 percent of the tickets are made available for Florida fans. But each contract is different, and only 6,500 were made available for Florida's first visit to 85,000-seat Kyle Field. Texas A&M, which wasn't used to such a high demand for tickets from an opponent, initially offered fewer, but Florida negotiated a higher availability. Here are the 13 SEC road games ranked in order of must-see:

## 1. Athens, Georgia (345 miles from Gainesville)

The problem is that Florida and Georgia play every year in Jacksonville, Florida. But the two schools did play in Athens in 1995, and it was one of those aforementioned stadium-emptying games.

**Why you should go:** Athens may have the most beautiful campus in the league with its rolling hills and foliage. Broad Street is a happening place with many restaurants and bars, and to see a game "between the hedges" is a historic experience. That famous phrase refers to the distinctive privet hedges, which ring the field at Sanford Stadium.

**Florida's record vs. Georgia in Athens:** 2–4.

## 2. Nashville, Tennessee (359 miles from Gainesville)

Because the Commodores are in the SEC East, this has become an every-other-year trip and one of the favorites for Gators fans.

**Why you should go:** Mainly because of Nashville. Music City is a fun place with a lively cultural and music scene, and the stadium isn't far from the action. The stadium itself isn't much, but there are usually plenty of places to sit. And Florida hasn't lost there since 1988.

**Florida's record vs. Vanderbilt in Nashville:** 16–7–1.

## 3. Columbia, South Carolina (359 miles from Gainesville)

This is one of those rivalries that was created by expansion and geography. Of the SEC cities the Gators visit every other year, only Auburn is closer to Gainesville than Columbia. The former coach vs. Florida backdrop piques interest as well.

**Why you should go:** It's in close proximity, which is a big plus especially for fans in Georgia and north Florida. The Five Points area is excellent, and make sure you stop at the Liberty Tap Room for a burger and a cold one.

**Florida's record vs. South Carolina in Columbia:** 10–5–1.

## 4. Baton Rouge, Louisiana (586 miles from Gainesville)

The LSU Tigers are Florida's permanent opponent from the SEC West, and the series has turned into one of college football's great rivalries.

**Why you should go:** Baton Rouge is nice, but Tiger Stadium makes this trip stand out. Visit Mike the Tiger—a live Bengal tiger in captivity—and tour the tailgating, which is an incredible scene.

**Florida's record vs. LSU in Baton Rouge:** 16–14.

## 5. Knoxville, Tennessee (544 miles from Gainesville)

Florida and Tennessee became serious rivals during the 1990s when Steve Spurrier and Phillip Fulmer had their teams among the elite of college football.

**Why you should go:** Knoxville is one of the bigger cities in the league, but the experience at Neyland Stadium will grab you. The Vol Navy storms up the Tennessee River to dock just outside the stadium, and the ribs next door at Calhoun's are first rate.

**Florida's record vs. Tennessee in Knoxville:** 11–11.

## 6. Oxford, Mississippi (618 miles from Gainesville)

Because Ole Miss is in the SEC West and not UF's permanent opponent, this game is only played every five or six years.

**Why you should go:** Oxford is a delightfully quaint city, but the highlight of this trip is The Grove, a huge tailgating area where fans rent tents and televisions to enhance their experience. You have to visit it.

**Florida's record vs. Ole Miss in Oxford:** 5–2.

## 7. Lexington, Kentucky (710 miles from Gainesville)

Florida has had amazing success in the Bluegrass State since 1992 when the game was moved from the latter part of the season—which often had cold air and hard ground—to the earlier part of the season.

**Why you should go:** If you are into horses, this is an SEC trip to take. The stadium is not far from Red Mile Race Track.

**Florida's record vs. Kentucky in Lexington:** 19–10.

## 8. Tuscaloosa, Alabama (450 miles from Gainseville)

The SEC's most-storied program has become a major rival for the Gators.

**Why you should go:** There is a lot of history in the stadium, and the tailgating is all over the campus. Just be prepared for a long wait to get out of the city.

**Florida's record vs. Alabama in Tuscaloosa:** 5–7

## 9. College Station, Texas (948 miles from Gainesville)

Florida played its first ever game at Kyle Field in 2012.

**Why you should go:** College Station isn't much, but seeing the pageantry of a game and feeling the stadium swaying back and forth should be experienced.

**Florida's record vs. Texas A&M in College Station:** 1–0.

## 10. Auburn, Alabama (310 miles from Gainesville)

The SEC discontinued this annual series when it changed the format after the 2002 season.

**Why you should go:** The village on the plains has some charm, but there is not a lot to do. The stadium is one of the best in the league, and watching the eagle soar down from the top of the stadium should be checked out.

**Florida's record vs. Auburn in Auburn: 8–26–1.**

## 11. Fayetteville, Arkansas (986 miles from Gainesville)

Florida played only one game against the Razorbacks prior to expansion, and that was the Bluebonnet Bowl in 1982.

**Why you should go:** There is a nice downtown strip, and the stadium is comfortable, but the media has facetiously dubbed it Fayette-Nam for a reason—as in you wouldn't want to go there.

**Florida's record vs. Arkansas in Fayetteville: 3–0.**

## 12. Starkville, Mississippi (535 miles from Gainesville)

Florida has a long tradition with the Bulldogs, but they rarely play these days.

**Why you should go:** Sarcastically referred to as Stark-Vegas—because Starkville has few attractions unlike Sin City—the town is getting better, but it lacks things to do and hotel space.

**Florida's record vs. Mississippi State in Starkville: 4–7.**

Note: I have not listed Columbia, Missouri, which is located 1,109 miles away from Gainesville, because I have yet to travel there for a Gators game. My first experience will be on October 19, 2013 when Florida plays its first game there.

# 83 The Norm Carlson Press Box

It was a festive night in a banquet room at the Reitz Union on the Florida campus in 2003. Some of the greatest players in the history of the program were there—guys like Jack Youngblood and Carlos Alvarez. Steve Spurrier was there, of course, because they were honoring one of his best friends in the world.

After celebrities and media people ended the night by expressing their love for Norm Carlson, the UF athletic director had a surprise. Jeremy Foley pulled out a plaque that told the story—the area where the media eats, works, and plays would be called the Norm Carlson Press Box. Now when anyone exits the elevators on the third floor of Ben Hill Griffin Stadium, the first thing you see in big block letters is—"Norm Carlson Press Box."

The sports information director for 40 years, Carlson retired in 2002. He helped Spurrier win a Heisman Trophy, saw coaches and players come and go, and offered young members of the media a kind word or a helping hand. He retired at age 69 but not completely. "I thought I retired," he said. But Foley talked Carlson into staying on as a historian, reducing his hours to the mornings. Carlson still writes for the game program and website, but mostly he answers questions about the past for the media or the SID staff.

And nobody knows the history of Florida football like Norm Carlson.

He graduated from UF in 1956 and worked at *The Atlanta Journal-Constitution* for two years before going to Auburn as the sports information director. But it was in Atlanta where he caught what he calls "one of the greatest breaks" in his life. He covered a high school football banquet at Druid Hills, an affluent section of

Atlanta, where Georgia Tech's defensive coordinator was speaking. That coordinator, Ray Graves, would be named the head coach at Florida in 1960, and the two made a real connection that night.

After the previous sports information director had been fired, Graves called Carlson in 1963, offering him a job back in Gainesville. Carlson jumped at the chance. "I remember [Auburn coach] Shug Jordan told me, 'You're making the right move,'" Carlson said. "You're going to your alma mater, and their resources are so much better than ours.'"

One of Carlson's first jobs at UF was to clean up the press box in Jacksonville, Florida's Gator Bowl. The game was played at a neutral site, but Florida was in charge of the press box. Gator Boosters and Jacksonville power brokers had taken it over for each game, stocking it with booze and other refreshments. Fans had started drinking in the press box while raucously cheering for their team. Graves had been hearing it from the media and told Carlson to get it fixed. "I told him I would, but he had to back me up," Carlson said. "I hired Pinkerton guards to keep anyone without a press pass out of the press box. I didn't see much of the game because there was such a fuss. But Coach Graves backed me up and we solved the problem."

In 1966 Carlson started what is believed to be the first Heisman campaign. "Nobody campaigned then, but Florida just wasn't on the football map," he said. "So I sent out fliers and releases on Steve Spurrier and talked some of the national writers into coming to see him play."

They came for the Auburn game where Spurrier kicked the game-winning field goal and eventually won the award. That was one of the highlights for Carlson. The lowlight occurred after the NCAA accused Charley Pell of breaking rules, and Florida fired him. "I liked Charley, and that was the hardest by far," Carlson said. "I remember that Charley wanted to have a press conference after he was fired. He didn't have to. And I remember walking him there to the room, and just before he walked in he turned to me and said, 'You know, Norm, you don't have to cheat to win at Florida.' And I said, 'No, Charley, you don't.'"

# 84 Galen Hall's Finale

It wasn't supposed to be a big game. LSU was struggling at 1–2, and Florida had managed three uneventful wins after an opening loss to Ole Miss. Neither team was ranked when they played in 1989. But there was something bubbling underneath the surface that would make this game memorable and not just because of the way it ended.

During the week leading up to the game, a Florida investigation had found some NCAA infractions against Hall. With the NCAA in town pursuing allegations against the basketball program, Florida already was in a state of turmoil. And with the football team still suffering from NCAA sanctions imposed four years earlier during Charley Pell's tenure, any breaking of the rules would be considered grounds for firing.

Florida's administration had let Hall know that this would be his last game. The head coach allegedly had sent money to Palatka, Florida, in 1987 for defensive back Jarvis Williams to pay child support. Hall denied the report, saying that the envelope contained some papers that Williams needed. It was also alleged that Hall had paid defensive coordinator Zaven Yaralian and offensive coordinator Lynn Amedee an extra supplement out of his pocket when they were at UF.

Word of Hall's firing remained quiet until *The Gainesville Sun* learned of the possibility during the week of the LSU game. *The Sun* sent two reporters to Hall's home, but he said he would only talk about it after the game. The players had no clue what was going on. They went to Tiger Stadium in Baton Rouge, Louisiana, simply trying to win their fourth straight game.

And it looked good for the Gators when Emmitt Smith broke a 19-yard touchdown run up the middle to give them a 13–10 lead with 13:41 to play in the game. But after a couple of changes in possession, LSU quarterback Tommy Hodson mounted a drive that would cover 41 yards. That led to a field goal, which tied the game with 1:41 to play. Florida got the ball back for one last try, and quarterback Kyle Morris found Smith on short passes that netted 12 and 6 yards. He then found wide receiver Ernie Mills for 18 yards and—after a sack—found Mills again for 18 yards.

Florida had a chance to kick the winning field goal but called one more play for Smith. Rather than go out of bounds to stop the clock, Smith cut inside to try to pick up extra yards. The problem was that Florida had no timeouts left. Morris hurried the team to the line of scrimmage and fired a pass out of bounds, but the clock read 0:00. Fireworks were set off over Tiger Stadium to signify the end of the game, but the officials ruled that one second should be put back on the clock.

John David Francis, Florida's regular field goal kicker, had made one field goal and missed another earlier in the game. Because of Francis' inconsistency, Hall turned to sophomore Arden Czyzewski in the third quarter. Czyzewski made his third-quarter try and was sent out to attempt the game-winner. His 41-yard kick barely squeaked inside the left upright, and the Gators started celebrating.

Hall was especially emotional after the win, and the players were surprised. The next day they would understand why. Florida called a press conference and announced Hall's dismissal. Gary Darnell, the defensive coordinator, took over the team on an interim basis.

Although Hall left in disgrace and struggled to get back into college coaching (he finished his career on Joe Paterno's last Penn State staff), his legacy was that of a coach who took over a difficult situation in 1984 when Charley Pell was fired. Hall won two SEC titles, even though neither was recognized because of NCAA sanctions, and his 1987 recruiting class became the core of the Steve Spurrier team that would win Florida's first official SEC crown in 1991.

# 85 The Heisman Replacements

There are three statues outside The Swamp. Three tributes to three Heisman Trophy winners. Three legendary Gators icons. The guys who replaced them know all about it.

For every great player in athletic history, there is someone who succeeds them. The old adage about how it's never good to replace a great coach, but it's better to replace the coach who replaces the great coach could apply to players as well—especially in the cases of Steve Spurrier, Danny Wuerffel, and Tim Tebow.

### Jackie Eckdahl

After Steve Spurrier's Heisman season in 1966, Florida had a local player ready to take his place at quarterback. Eckdahl starred at Gainesville High, but he was more of an option quarterback than the pro-style quarterback fitting Florida's system.

After spending his freshman season learning from Spurrier, Eckdahl was the heir apparent. In the 1967 opener against Illinois, UF coach Ray Graves wanted to ease Eckdahl into the position. He started with Harmon Wages at quarterback and had Eckdahl play one series in the first half. But in the second half, the keys were handed to Eckdahl. He responded by leading Florida to a pair of touchdown drives in a 14–0 victory. But in the third game of the season, Eckdahl suffered a broken leg. Converted safety Larry Rentz took his place. "Having the opportunity to be a Gators quarterback, that's huge," Eckdahl said. "To step in and start some games, I consider that one of the highlights of my life. There was some [pressure] for sure. But I think once you go out there and get knocked around a few times, that kind of goes out the window. You turn your focus to doing what it takes to win games."

In 1968 both Rentz and Eckdahl played the position with Eckdahl throwing for 572 yards and Rentz for 533. For Eckdahl's senior season, Graves chose to go with sophomore John Reaves, and Eckdahl was moved to defense. "I was disappointed," Eckdahl said. "But when I look back on my Florida career, it was a positive."

## Doug Johnson

Like Eckdahl, Johnson was a local guy, having been a star baseball and football player at Buchholz High. He stepped in after Wuerffel's senior season and led the Gators to a 5–0 start and the No. 1 ranking in 1997.

But a loss at LSU derailed Florida's hopes for a repeat. And the following week, Johnson was suspended for missing curfew. He would alternate at the position the rest of the year—and the rest of his career—with both Noah Brindise and Jesse Palmer. "With Danny it wasn't just trying to replace the player—but replacing the guy," Johnson said. "He was such a phenomenal human being. It was a lot, but looking back you're so busy preparing that you don't realize how difficult it was. It was different then, too. Today Gators fans wonder if they are going to win big games. Then it was, *How much are we going to win by?*"

Injuries also became an issue for Johnson. He suffered a shoulder injury in the Citrus Bowl during his sophomore year and a leg injury in the Orange Bowl the following season. And he missed all but three plays of the SEC Championship Game in 1999 with a sore throwing shoulder. "Once you leave you take a breath and look back," Johnson said. "And you say, 'Wow, that was some ride.'"

Johnson's last game as the Florida quarterback was a Citrus Bowl loss to Michigan State, but it was one of his best games as he threw for 288 yards and three touchdowns.

## John Brantley

Think it was difficult to follow Spurrier or Wuerffel? Try following Tebow. That was the job given to Brantley, who waited patiently for his chance to be the Florida quarterback, finally receiving the opportunity as a junior.

He shied away from all the attention, saying, "I'm just a dude from Ocala." But as a backup to Tebow, he showed his ability to be a big-time passer. So expectations were high when he took over the job.

Brantley was a drop-back passer, but Florida was still running a version of the spread option offense that made Tebow a legend. Brantley managed to lead Florida to a 4–0 start in 2010, but he suffered cracked ribs, a sore shoulder, and a bruised thumb during a loss to Alabama. Florida lost its next two games and lost the SEC East title when South Carolina won in The Swamp. Brantley was contemplating a transfer, but Meyer resigned, and Will Muschamp became the Florida coach. He hired Charlie Weis to be his offensive coordinator, and Brantley decided to stay for his senior year.

*Faced with the tough task of succeeding Heisman Trophy winner Danny Wuerffel, quarterback Doug Johnson threw for 7,114 yards and 62 touchdowns during his Florida career.*

## Doug Johnson's Numbers

Despite his on-again, off-again quarterback status during his Florida career, Doug Johnson put up some impressive numbers from 1996 to 1999.

- His 57 pass attempts in the 1997 game against LSU are the second most in Florida history.
- His 7,114 yards passing are the ninth most ever at UF.
- His seven touchdown passes against Central Michigan in 1997 are tied for the most ever thrown by a Gators quarterback in one game.
- His 62 career touchdown passes rank sixth on the UF all-time list.
- His 20 games of throwing for more than 200 yards are seventh in UF history, and his seven 300-yard games rank fourth.

It started out well with four straight wins, but again Alabama was the culprit. In a 38–10 loss, Brantley left the game with a severely sprained ankle. Brantley sat while Florida lost its next two games before returning with a heavily taped ankle for the Georgia game. He led Florida to a 17–3 lead, but the Bulldogs rallied for a 24–20 win. Brantley suffered a concussion in a loss to Florida State before quarterbacking Florida's Gator Bowl win against Ohio State.

# 86 Special Returners

Florida's football history is filled with special teams players who made some special plays. Who is the best returner in UF history? There are plenty of candidates, and they span several decades.

Not many of you (if any) are old enough to remember Hal Griffin. But during his 1946 season, Griffin returned three punts that year of 75 yards or longer. And if that wasn't enough, he set an NCAA record for punt return average when he averaged 26.7 yards a return the following year. Loren Broadus ran back a punt for 80 yards in 1947 and then repeated that feat the next year.

Jim Rountree had a huge kickoff return in Florida's 19–13 win against Georgia in 1955, taking one back 85 yards. One of the best punt returners to ever play at Florida was All-American cornerback Steve Tannen. He ran two punts back for scores in 1968. Willie Jackson Sr. is second all-time in Florida history in kickoff returns, running them back for 1,248 yards from 1970 to 1972. Ivory Curry and Ricky Nattiel were exciting punt returners in the 1980s, and Bo Carroll and Reidel Anthony excelled as kick returners in the 1990s. Lito Sheppard had a signature moment in 2000 when he returned a punt 57 yards for a score as the first half expired against South Carolina, leaving Gamecocks coach Lou Holtz aghast on the

## The Longest Yards
Florida's five longest punt and kickoff returns in school history:

### Kickoff returns
100—Andre Debose vs. Louisville in 2013
100—Bo Carroll at LSU in 1999
100—Jack Jackson vs. Mississippi State in 1993
100—Pat Reen at Miami in 1940
99—Andre Debose vs. Ohio State in 2011 and vs. South Carolina in 2010, Jeff Demps vs. Georgia in 2011, and Tony Lomack vs. Kentucky in 1989

### Punt returns
97—Hal Griffin vs. Miami in 1946
87—Hal Griffin vs. Villanova in 1946
86—Jacquez Green at South Carolina in 1997
84—Loren Broadus vs. Rollins in 1948
83—Brandon James vs. Tennessee in 2007, George Gandy vs. Tulane in 1966

sideline. And current Gators returner Andre Debose has the UF record for kickoff returns for touchdowns with four, including one in the 2013 Sugar Bowl.

But among all those great Gators returners, two players brought the crowd to their feet every time they touched the ball—Jacquez Green and Brandon James. Green had an innate ability to make the first guy miss and then several more after that on punt returns. His two returns for touchdowns (covering 66 and 79 yards) against Kentucky were spectacular enough. But after the game, Gator Nation learned Green suffered from asthma as he was almost suffocated by celebrating teammates after his second score. Green finished his career with four punt returns for touchdowns and 766 yards in punt returns. He also returned kickoffs in 1995 and 1996 (and suffered a dislocated hip on a kickoff return in the 1996 Fiesta Bowl).

Although Green was known more for his punt returns, James was known for both. He has the career record for kickoff return yardage with 2,718 and punt return yardage with 1,371. "He had a tremendous first step," said Urban Meyer, who emphasized special teams more than any other Florida coach. "That's what made him different."

James and Green are tied for the Florida record with four punt return touchdowns each. James also had a kickoff return for a score. He has the top three totals in kickoff return yardage for a season and two of the top three for punt return yardage. He is also the only player to lead Florida in punt return yards and kickoff return yards for four straight years.

# 87 Walk the Locker Room Halls

It may take a connection or two, but if a Florida football fan has the chance to tour the locker room area in the south end zone of The Swamp, it will be like touring a museum.

Florida had one of the SEC's worst locker rooms before Charley Pell raised money for improvements when he became the Florida coach in 1979. Each coach since has added touches, but Urban Meyer, knowing that high school recruits could be influenced by their working conditions, added the biggest change. After he pushed for an upgrade, a $28 million project (all of it coming from private donors) that included the Heavener Complex and also enhanced the locker room area was completed in 2008.

Will Muschamp has added his own touches in the form of posters and slogans. You can't walk anywhere without an inspirational message staring you in the face. In the main meeting room, one reads, "This is a statement game." In the hallways one reads, "Boys do what they want to do. Men do what they have to do." In the locker room, one reads, "Graduate With a Degree." And in the weight room, it reads, "Why Not Me? Do the Little Things Right."

The hallways converge at a foyer where the team gathers before taking the field. A giant alligator head is perched on a table, and the players touch it for good luck before heading onto the field. Those hallways also serve as an amazing tribute to Gators history. Each of the three national championship seasons are commemorated in a glassed-in display that includes national championship trophies. Although the crystal ball trophies are located in the Heavener Complex, other awards—such as the Associated Press National Championship Trophy—are located in these displays. Another glassed-in display shows the rings from the national titles. Above those rings a television blasts highlights from great Gators games of the past.

On one of the walls, all of the Florida players who have been named All-SEC are honored. On another wall all of the Gators first-round draft picks are shown with mini-helmets of the teams that drafted them. Each SEC championship team is also honored. The displays are up for a reason. They showcase the Gators football tradition to recruits and let current players know what is expected of them.

The complex has half a dozen meeting rooms, including a main one that doubles as a media area after games or for important press conferences. The chairs are upholstered with orange-and-blue cloth that resembles alligator skin. And if you can sneak upstairs to the coaches' offices (which were also redone in 2008), you will see more displays honoring great Gators of the past. With all of this luxury (the lounge in the players' locker room features oversized chairs and couches), the players and coaches are still able to get some work done.

It is somewhat ironic that the biggest locker room upgrades occurred under Meyer's watch. When he first became the Florida coach in 2005, he booted the players out of the locker room. They weren't allowed to dress there or use any of the facilities and had to wear their own gear during voluntary workouts, leading up to that spring practice. Meyer felt the team had to earn the right to wear Florida clothes and use the Florida facilities. He even had the alligator head removed.

When word leaked out about his method, it upset Meyer, but the players eventually were allowed back into the locker room. And the alligator head was returned to its rightful spot.

# 88 The Work 'Em Silly Sign

Pete Calamore wanted to do something for his first big game as a University of Florida student. So the freshman jumped on a friend's bike and rode to the Salvation Army. He purchased a bed sheet, bought some spray paint at Wal-Mart, and a Gators tradition was born.

Calamore made a sign that day in 1993 that read simply, "Work 'Em Silly." Although the sign has been through several reincarnations, it remains a staple at Florida football games. "It seemed like the college thing to do," Calamore said. "And it hasn't missed a home game since."

Calamore, who now works on the UF campus at the College of Health and Human Performance, also takes the sign on the road when he goes. But he doesn't make as many games as he used to because he and his wife, Laura, have two young sons.

Maybe it's just as well. The sign has seen better days at home than on the road. At LSU in 1997, Calamore and his friends decided to take it over to the LSU student section. "Someone snatched it and took it into the students," he said. "It was in shreds within seconds. Maybe that was a good thing because they beat us, and they'd have been able to parade the sign around after the game."

At the 1993 SEC Championship Game in Birmingham, Alabama, someone working the game at Legion Field took the sign down and took it to the other side of the stadium. "My friend watched to see the trash can he put it into and went and got it," Calamore said.

He estimates that the sign that hangs at The Swamp now is the fifth one he has created. He used to take it to basketball games as well, but since he's unable to attend all of the home games, he stopped bringing the sign. He once took it to an NCAA women's tennis championship in Tallahassee, only to have to fetch it back from a Stanford player.

The sign's current spot is in the northwest corner of the end zone draped over the orange wall. "I still consider it first-come, first-serve," Calamore said. "They have a policy that no signs are allowed, but my theory is that unless it's inappropriate or covers up some of the letters on the wall, they are going to allow it [at the stadium]."

Allow it? The "Work 'Em Silly" sign has become a staple of Gator gamedays. When Calamore and his friends were at the Fiesta Bowl in 1996, Steve Spurrier's wife, Jerri, told him she always looked for the sign when she came into whatever stadium where the Gators were playing.

So what does "Work 'Em Silly" mean?

"The lingo comes from the Jerky Boys," Calamore said. "At the time it was something we found funny because of the way they talked. It just means to work harder than the other guys. But people didn't know what it meant for a couple of years."

Calamore used to wear an orange-and-blue bandanna to games and acquired the nickname "Bandanna Pete." And there is a bit of celebrity status that goes with being the guy responsible for a Gators tradition. "I don't know how I'd quantify it," he said. "Every now and then, people will ask me questions while I'm putting it up. I also get people who tell me that I'm wrong about the year that I started it. They insist that it was up long before 1993. If someone sent me a picture of a game before then with the sign, I'd probably freak out."

# 89 Visit the Touchdown Terrace

When Florida decided to expand the stadium before the 1991 season, it involved more than simply putting in some more seats to increase the capacity up to 83,000. While the seats already in the north end zone remained and new seats were added that reached high into the air (known as the Sunshine Seats), the centerpiece of the expansion was sandwiched between those rows of bleachers.

The Touchdown Terrace was the jewel of the new construction. It has become more than a place to watch the games. And while more recent expansion has produced the Champions Club on the west side, the end zone suites that are part of the Touchdown Terrace remain full.

Those 18 suites—called the Gator Dens— include microwaves, sinks, bars, and refrigerators for Gators fans who want to enjoy the game in comfort. Each Gator Den seats 20 people, and those fans are treated to a buffet lunch before the game. It's not cheap. It costs $56,000 for one of the suites for a football season.

Below those Dens there are almost 2,000 special Touchdown Terrace seats, which have access to the lounge and televisions showing replays. Those seats cost $2,200 a season plus the cost of the game tickets. The lounge for the Touchdown Terrace includes two exclusive concession stands and bathrooms. There are couches and chairs for fans to use before the game, at halftime, or just to take a mid-game break.

Even though it's a rear view of the action, the Touchdown Terrace has become a popular place for fans who want to enjoy the luxury of a suite. But it's more than that. And for a Gators fan who has a sense of history, you could get lost on the wall, which backs up to the suites. There are plaques (with pictures) of every member of the Florida Athletic Hall of Fame for every sport. They were moved there when the Terrace opened. Before 1991 they were located in the old F Club at Gate 15.

Each year the Hall of Fame banquet is held in the Terrace where a half dozen or so Gator greats are honored at a black-tie affair. Florida also holds its football banquet as well as banquets for other sports in the Terrace. Florida's preseason media day is also held there with players occupying the suites for interviews. Several charity events take place at the Terrace each year.

# The New SEC

The powerful organization now generates hundred of millions of dollars to distribute to its member schools. But when it started, the Southeastern Conference was a spinoff. The roots of the conference go all the way back to the first conference ever founded for college sports—the Southern Intercollegiate Athletic Association. That conference formed on December 22, 1894 in Atlanta, and the first SIAA included current SEC members Alabama, Auburn, Georgia, and Vanderbilt.

The SIAA became so popular that it swelled to 30 teams by 1920. But teams from the same conference weren't playing each other, and it felt less like a conference than a collection of teams. Disagreements about freshmen eligibility and summer semipro baseball also arose. As a result 11 teams split from the SIAA and formed the Southern Conference. That conference saw its ranks expand rapidly, and by 1932 there were 23 members.

## Easy Giants Trivia
### Questions
1. Who was the first commissioner of the SEC?
2. Where was the first SEC Championship Game played, and who played in it?
3. Which two teams played in the first televised SEC game?
4. Which two teams played in the first ever SEC game?
5. Who won the SEC's first championship?

**Answers**
1. Former Mississippi governor Martin S. Conner served from 1940 to 1946;
2. Alabama defeated Florida 28–21 at Legion Field in Birmingham, Alabama;
3. Tennessee defeated Alabama 27–13 in 1951; 4. Kentucky defeated Sewanee 7–0 in 1933; 5. Alabama won in 1933 with a 5–0–1 record.

So the school presidents met in Knoxville, Tennessee, and they formed another split. The 12 schools to the west and south of the Appalachian Mountains created a new conference—the Southeastern Conference. The original members were: Alabama, Auburn, Georgia, Georgia Tech, Florida, LSU, Kentucky, Ole Miss, Mississippi State, Sewanee, Tennessee, Tulane, and Vanderbilt.

It didn't take long for Sewanee (also known as the University of the South) to realize it was in over its head. The school pulled out of the SEC in 1940 without ever winning a conference game. Georgia Tech had issues with the other schools oversigning high school recruits and withdrew in 1964 to become an independent. Tulane pulled out in 1966 to become independent as well. That left the SEC as the one so many Gator fans grew up with—a 10-team league dominated by Alabama and Georgia. From 1966 to 1991, the Tide won or shared 10 SEC titles, and Georgia won or shared six.

But in the early 1990s, SEC commissioner Roy Kramer had an idea. If the league had a championship game, it could generate millions of extra dollars. To field a championship game, the league would have to expand to 12. And if it were to expand, why not augment the geographic footprint as well? So the league brought in Arkansas and South Carolina, two schools in states that did not have SEC teams. South Carolina had been a member of the Southern Conference but left to help form the Atlantic Coast Conference in 1953. The school then left the ACC in 1971 to become an independent. Arkansas had been a charter member of the Southwest Conference.

The 12-team SEC paved the way for future conference championship games and also showed that a bloated conference wouldn't stand in the way of national glory. Since the expansion to 12 teams, the league has won 10 national titles in football. But the league was not finished. As the college football revolution began to overpower conference loyalty like a tsunami of greed, the SEC was patient. Teams were jumping from conference to conference, but SEC commissioner Mike Slive knew exactly what he needed—two more footprints in states where there were no SEC teams to help build the SEC Network.

That eliminated schools such as Florida State, Clemson, Georgia Tech, and Louisville. Instead in 2012 the league turned to the high school hotbed of Texas to lure Texas A&M and then to Missouri to convince the Tigers to come to the league. The 14-team league was set.

# 91 The Golden Era

The 1990s were golden as Steve Spurrier won like no coach before him. The Gators captured five SEC championships and a national title. The decade from 2000 to 2009 was also golden with Spurrier winning another SEC crown and Urban Meyer winning a pair of national titles. But only one period of Gator football is known as "The Golden Era."

And it is the most ironic of titles, which is the point.

The name was bestowed on the period after World War II and through the end of the 1940s. Jimmy Kynes, a two-way player and All-SEC center who went on to become the attorney general for the state of Florida, is given credit for the name. "He and Red Mitchum [who played in 1950 and 1951] were the ones who pretty much came up with it," UF historian Norm Carlson said.

It was hardly golden. But from it sprang a cohesiveness among the former players from that time who still hold reunions and have raised money for scholarships and facility improvements over the years. In 1943 Florida's football team was so depleted by the war effort that UF did not field a team. When they started playing again in '44, the Gators were mostly a group of players, who had returned from the war and hadn't played football in a while. After two seasons of four wins each, Thomas Lieb was fired and replaced by Raymond "Bear" Wolf.

Florida lost the final game of the 1945 season to the U.S. Amphibs in Norfolk, Virginia. That was the real beginning of the Golden Era. Florida would lose all nine games the next year and three to start the 1947 season. The 13-game losing streak was unparalleled in UF history.

Hence the ironic name.

The losses included a 47–12 defeat to Auburn in Gainesville, which closed the 1946 season. But it wasn't as if Florida was blown out in every game during the streak. Six of the losses came by a margin of eight points or less. Florida broke the streak with a win against No. 18 North Carolina State. Bobby Forbes' 70-yard touchdown run fueled that 7–6 victory.

But after five seasons and a 13–24–2 record, Wolf was fired. His bright spot was a 28–7 win against Georgia in 1949 when

Charlie Hunsinger ran for 174 yards and three touchdowns. Bob Woodruff was hired to replace Wolf, and Florida football started a slow climb back to respectability.

It wasn't as if Florida did not have any good players during that era, but it only managed three SEC wins from 1945 to 1949. And during this time—1946 to be exact—George Edmondson began his "Mr. Two Bits" routine.

The bond forged by the players from those teams, however, has lasted through the decades that have followed—a testament to the old saying that adversity doesn't build character but reveals it. "The main things holding us together over this long period of time have been our love for each other and the University of Florida," Kynes told Carlson before the attorney general passed away from stomach cancer in 1988.

# 92 The Florida-Auburn Rivalry

When the SEC changed its scheduling format in 2002, it took away one of the great annual rivalries in the conference. Florida and Auburn had been playing each other on their respective campuses since 1950. It was the easiest trip for Gators fans, a mere five-hour drive from Gainesville, and Auburn fans always filled their allotted seats for the games in Gainesville.

But since 2002 the two teams have only played three times. Florida lost to Auburn in 2011 but was robbed of a chance to get revenge in 2012. When the league expanded to 14 teams in 2012, it changed all of the schedules in the league and prevented some rivals from meeting annually.

Prior to the 1950 season, the two teams played in a variety of places. The first game was played in 1912 at Auburn, and the Tigers won the first six games of the rivalry. Florida and Auburn played in Jacksonville, Florida; Montgomery, Alabama; Miami; Columbus, Georgia; Tampa, Florida; and Mobile, Alabama, prior to 1950. They first played as ranked teams in 1957 when Auburn won 13–0 on its way to the national championship.

Since then they have played a number of memorable games against each other. In 1966 Steve Spurrier kicked the winning field goal during a 30–27 Florida victory, which basically earned him the Heisman Trophy. There was the nine-interception game when the Tigers ended Florida's unbeaten season in 1969. And Florida's 24–19 victory in Gainesville in 1976 included one of

## The Streak Is Over

Heading into the 1973 game, Florida had never won at Auburn, and there was no reason to think that year would be any different. The Gators had lost four in a row, and Auburn was ranked 19th. But at Jordan-Hare Stadium, the Tigers would face a different Florida team.

During the bye week, UF coach Doug Dickey had changed the offense and worked with backup quarterback Don Gaffney on more option and sprint-out plays. The team, though, didn't know that it would be Gaffney, a sophomore from Jacksonville, who would lead Florida to its first win at Auburn.

In the locker room before the game, Dickey handed Gaffney the football and said, "You got it." A few lockers away, defensive back Wayne Fields said, "It's about time."

Florida also moved Jimmy DuBose to fullback and Vince Kendrick to tailback. The Gators dominated the game, though a late Gaffney fumble made the 12–8 score closer than it seemed. Gaffney, the first African American to start at quarterback, was in tears after the game because he had cost the defense a shutout.

It didn't matter. The streak was over.

the greatest catch-and-run plays in Florida history. Wes Chandler took a short pass from quarterback Jimmy Fisher and juked three Auburn defenders before scoring on a 64-yard reception. As he crossed the goal line, someone from Auburn finally got a piece of him—the War Eagle. The school's mascot jumped from his perch and grabbed Chandler by the shoulder pads as he scored.

The rivalry became especially intense in the mid-1980s. Both teams were ranked in the top five in 1983 when Auburn won 28–21 on a controversial Neal Anderson fumble. When both were ranked in the top 13 the next year, Florida got revenge with a 24–3 win. The following year, Florida was ranked second and Auburn sixth when Florida won 14–10. The victory propelled UF to its first No. 1 ranking.

The series became even more intriguing during the 1990s. Terry Bowden took over as the Auburn quarterback and twice upset the Gators. The question arose as to whether Spurrier could beat a Bowden (since he had won only one of his first five games against Terry's father, Florida State coach Bobby Bowden). Spurrier's 1995 team won in the rain on the plains on its way to the national title game.

The rivalry died down in the late 1990s as Florida dominated by winning seven in a row, including the 2000 SEC Championship Game. But in 2001 Auburn stunned the No. 1 Gators 23–20 on a late field goal.

Urban Meyer had only two shots at the Tigers, and both ended badly. Auburn beat No. 2 Florida in 2006 and appeared to cripple UF's shot at a national title, though the Gators rebounded to win it all. In 2007 a last-second field goal gave Auburn the 20–17 victory.

# 93 Check Out the F Club

When expansion plans were being drawn up for the north end zone in 1990, there was a proposal that a football museum be included. Although that idea was nixed, the F Club is the next best thing.

The meeting room is located at the entrance to the north end zone on the ground floor below the office of the Gator Boosters. It has two main purposes on gamedays. Several hours before home games, it hosts the parents of players on the football team. And just before the home games and at halftime, it hosts lettermen of all UF sports. For all these groups, it's an opportunity for both groups to mingle, eat, and drink.

Though used by the University Athletic Association and the occasional charity organization for meetings, the F Club is more than a meeting room. Historic photos cover the walls of the F Club. Newspapers dating back to when the university was located in Lake City are framed along with pictures of old Gators teams. A framed picture of the 1996 national championship team meeting President Bill Clinton rests on the east wall. Glass trophy cases contain all kinds of memorabilia. Among the items are a leather helmet and jersey from the 1928 team, a Gators helmet signed by Emmitt Smith, and Steve Spurrier's No. 11 game jersey.

The inside is just part of the experience of the north end zone building. As you walk to the front door, an 8-foot bronze alligator mounted on a 3-foot granite slab greets you. A gift from boosters Warren Cason, Stumpy Harris, and Jeffrey Ulmer in honor of the 1996 team, the alligator was placed at the stadium on April 4, 1998. Florida fans as well as students love to get their pictures taken with the alligator.

From the bronze alligator, you cross the Courtyard of Champions to enter the F Club. The courtyard is a series of bricks that commemorate endowment donations to Gator Boosters by former Gator athletes. Former football stars such as Jack Jackson and Mike Pearson have bricks in the courtyard.

Through the glass doors, a foyer includes another alligator statue. This one depicts two small alligators fighting and is called "Dueling Gators." The east wall lists the winners of the Ben Hill Griffin Award, which has gone to the top male and female Gator athletes since 1992. Upstairs is the office of the Gator Boosters; millions of dollars are raised there annually.

Straight ahead is the F Club, but it's not open to the public. So you have three choices. You can play a sport at UF (and thus qualify for membership into the club), you can have a child who plays football for the Gators, or you can know someone who will give you a tour.

## 94 Rent Albert and Alberta

Although Florida's football program is more than 100 years old and the Gators name was coined before World War I, the uniformed mascots are much younger.

It wasn't until 1970 that Florida put someone in an alligator costume to parade around the field at Gators games. Before that a wooden alligator was dragged around on the field in the 1940s, and during the 1950s, a live alligator had been housed in a chain-link pen. Two of those alligators died.

In 1970 Albert the Alligator began to walk on two legs. The first costume looked a lot like the cartoon character Pogo with a giant head and two huge eyes. In 1979 Disney made a $5,000 leather costume for a student to wear to games. But that didn't last long because of Florida's heat and humidity. In 1984 Florida introduced the Albert you see today. Some fans referred to him as "Fat Albert" because of his bulging waistline. It was two years later that he received some company when Florida introduced a female version named Alberta. The two have become so popular that there are life-sized bronze statues of them near Emerson Alumni Hall. The statues, erected in 2003, serve as a popular stop for students and fans wanting to pose for photos.

The mascot's main job is to cheer on the Gators at different sporting events—baseball's version is named Al—but they can be rented for different functions, though it is pricey and has restrictions. Albert and Alberta cannot be rented out for private weddings or parties nor taken outside Alachua County. However, you can rent them for a birthday party if it takes place on site before a Florida sporting event. For obvious reasons (it gets warm inside those suits), Albert and Alberta each receive a pair of 10-minute breaks every hour. Here are the hourly prices.

- For Albert or Alberta, it costs $350.
- For Albert and Alberta, it costs $550.
- For the cheerleaders or the Dazzlers (Florida's dance group), it costs $350.
- For Albert or Alberta and the cheerleaders or Dazzlers, it costs $450.
- For Albert, Alberta, and the cheerleaders, or the Dazzlers, it costs $550.
- For everybody, it costs $700.

"Fall is the busiest time," said Casey Reed, the Dazzler and mascot coordinator at UF. "They average one appearance a day outside of the regular sporting events. In the spring it drops off to about one appearance a week."

*For a $450 payment, you can have Albert—the Florida mascot—and cheerleaders appear at your birthday party.*

Prices are reduced for official UF events. Each charity can have a free appearance by Albert and Alberta once a year (with a $5 request fee), and each elementary school can have them appear once a year for free.

Albert has become one of the most popular mascots in college sports, even appearing in a *SportsCenter* commercial when the late Steve Irwin, the Crocodile Hunter, wrestled him to the ground.

# Jason Odom and Other Blocks of Granite

Jason Odom just laughs when you ask him about the Jacobs Blocking Trophy. "Someone was asking me the other day about trophies," he said. "And I told them about the Jacobs Award. I never saw a trophy or a plaque. I think I got some kind of piece of paper rolled up, but I don't even know where that is now. But it was still a great honor."

The award given to the conference's best blocker began in 1933 in honor of William P. Jacobs, the founder of Presbyterian College. It was presented by his two sons to linemen in the state of South Carolina until 1933 when the Southern Conference began giving the award. The SEC started giving out Jacobs Trophies in 1935 with Riley Smith of Alabama winning the award.

One of five Gators to have been named the SEC's best blocker by the league's coaches, Odom was a two-time winner of the award. The Florida left tackle won in both 1994 and 1995. For Odom, it was a baptism by fire. He was thrust into the lineup in 1992 as a true freshman. Florida also started the year with another true freshman Reggie Green at left tackle. After two straight losses, Odom

## Other Notable Florida O-Linemen

Florida has had five Jacobs Trophy winners, but several others were candidates for the honor. Here are five All-Americans who did not win the award, which is given to the SEC's best blocking lineman.

### 1. John Barrow

Barrow was voted the SEC's Lineman of the Year by the writers in 1956, but the Jacobs Trophy went to Stockton Adkins of Tennessee.

### 2. Larry Gagner

Gagner was a physical tackle in 1965 who would eventually start for the Pittsburgh Steelers and Kansas City Chiefs in the NFL, but the award went to Hal Wantland of Tennessee.

### 3. Guy Dennis

Dennis was one of the best guards to ever play at UF, but the award in 1968 went to Brad Johnson of Georgia.

### 4. Burton Lawless

Lawless, a big part of Florida's success in 1974, went on to a career with the Dallas Cowboys, but the award went to Sylvester Croom of Alabama.

### 5. Maurkice Pouncey

Pouncey was the center on two teams that won 26 games combined and a national title, but the 2009 award went to Ciron Black of LSU.

was inserted at right tackle against LSU. "Rick McGeorge was our offensive line coach and he always had me working with the first team," Odom said. "So I felt like it was going to happen. I just didn't know where or when."

Odom played right tackle the rest of the season as Florida reached the SEC Championship Game. He played there again as a sophomore before switching to left tackle as a junior. "There is nothing that could replace the experience I got by starting that early," Odom said. "When you're 19 years old, you're not thinking about a whole lot of anything anyway."

Odom was Florida's only two-time winner of the award, but the year after Odom graduated, right guard Donnie Young won it, making it a three-peat for the Gators. Young also played some at tackle and served as a leader on the national championship team in 1996. At Vanderbilt that year, the Commodores almost ruined the Gators' season with a rally that cut the Florida lead to 28–21. Facing a fourth-and-1 in their own territory, the Gators went for it. Young told quarterback Danny Wuerffel to follow him and he'd make sure Florida converted. They did and were able to run out the clock.

Lomas Brown, perhaps the best Florida offensive linemen ever, was the first Gators player to win the award. He did so in 1984 when the Gators won their first SEC title—only to have their title stripped away the following spring. An imposing left tackle, Brown went on to have a long career in the NFL.

Florida won its first official SEC title in 1991, and Cal Dixon was the second Jacobs winner. The center anchored an offensive line that helped Florida produce 457 yards a game. Left tackle Kenyatta Walker, who won the award in 2000, is the only other player to earn the award.

The Atlantic Coast Conference, the South Atlantic Conference, and the Southern Conference all give out Jacobs Trophies. Barrett Jones of Alabama won the 2012 SEC award. Other winners have included Michael Oher of Ole Miss, John Hannah of Alabama, and Chip Kell of Tennessee.

# 96 Places to Find Real Gators

Outside the Southeast, there is an urban legend that Floridians have to be careful going to their cars each morning because they might step on an alligator. In truth alligators can be nuisances, showing up in someone's pool or the suburban pond, but those cases are rare.

Although every golf course worth its salt has a few gators living in its ponds, you usually see them only when they sun themselves on the banks. But if you want to catch the namesake of the Florida football team, Gainesville has two prime spots for viewing the scaly beasts.

Lake Alice, the largest lake on the Florida campus, is home to all kinds of wildlife. (That includes a bathhouse where people

### Here Come the Gators

The alligators—the real life ones—are such a big part of the Florida football experience that they receive their share of video time before each game.

Until 1988 Florida's players came running onto the field to the band playing and the fans cheering. But everything changed in 1998 when UF put up state-of-the-art video boards in both end zones. Now a video shows alligators in their environment, swimming after prey and gliding into the water from a grassy bank. The message is simple, and it echoes throughout the stadium as a large alligator opens his mouth as an eerie invitation—"The Swamp…Only Gators Get Out Alive!"

That's when the members of the team run out onto the field. As they do, the pre-recorded voice of Jim Finch, the PA announcer from 1966 until his death in 2002, welcomes them with, "Heeerrreee come the Gators!"

gather at dusk to watch bats take off for their nocturnal feedings.) Students walking the path next to the lake are sometimes startled by an alligator resting only a few feet away.

One of the signature photos by noted Florida photographer John Moran is of Lake Alice just as the sun sets. Moran's photo captures thousands of alligator eyes reflecting the setting sun. At the Meditation Center, a building located at the southwest corner of the lake, people spend time enjoying the view and occasionally get married there.

As many alligators as there are at Lake Alice, it pales in comparison to Payne's Prairie. Florida's first state preserve is just minutes south of the campus. There are observation decks off the two main highways that cut through the 21,000-acre preserve, but if you really want to see a lot of gators, go on a walking tour during the day. The gators are especially plentiful in the afternoons when the sun is out.

# 97 Wilber Marshall and Other Defensive Studs

There are only two defensive players in the Ring of Honor—linebacker Wilber Marshall and defensive end Jack Youngblood, and because of the Ring's restrictive requirements, it's going to be difficult for other defensive players to join them. But it's not because Florida has been a wasteland for defensive talent. It's quite the opposite in fact.

You can go back into the history of the program to find players such as Charlie LaPradd, Fergie Ferguson, and Vel Heckman. Or you can look at the recent history with players such as Brandon

Spikes, Brandon Siler, and Reggie Nelson. Was Marshall the best defensive player ever at Florida? Was Youngblood? They'd certainly be in the discussion.

Marshall came to Florida as a tight end but was converted to outside linebacker. He finished his career with 343 tackles in three seasons and 23 sacks. Those totals have him in the top 10 in both categories on Florida's all-time list, but one eye-popping statistic is why many consider him the best defender in UF history. During his Florida career, Marshall had 58 tackles for a loss.

Youngblood lacks Marshall's numbers because they didn't keep those kinds of statistics when he played from 1968 to 1970. They didn't officially record sacks in the NFL until 1982, which delayed Youngblood's induction into the Hall of Fame. Every year the writer assigned to present Youngblood's case to the other voters would find himself in an argument over sacks he credited to Youngblood.

Sometimes a player's successful NFL career elevates his status as a college player, and that may be the case with both Marshall and Youngblood. It also is one reason you won't hear too many arguments for players such as Alonzo Johnson and Clifford Charlton. Both of those linebackers were NFL busts after being tenacious college players. Charlton has the Florida record with 15 forced fumbles and also had 49 tackles for a loss during his career from 1984 to 1987. Johnson had 55 tackles for a loss from 1981 to 1985, the second highest total in UF history.

But how do you compare a pass-rushing end like Alex Brown (school record 33 sacks) and a lockdown cornerback like Fred Weary (school record 15 interceptions)? Or a disruptive force like tackle Ellis Johnson with a middle linebacker like Scot Brantley, David Little, or Sammy Green?

You take a player like Spikes, who had four career interception returns for touchdowns from the middle linebacker position, and compare him with a cornerback like Steve Tannen, an All-American in 1969. It doesn't work. They're two different players from two different eras. Spikes was a 6'5" linebacker; Tannen was a 5'10" cornerback.

Keiwan Ratliff has the UF record for most interceptions in a season with nine. In 1970 John Clifford set the record with seven interceptions during a time when teams were much more run-oriented. Florida's football history is laced with players such as these. And with a defensive-minded head coach like Will Muschamp now running the show, there are certainly more to come.

# 98 The Cocktail Party's RV City

There are many wonders of the world (some say seven), but one of them truly has to be RV City in Jacksonville, Florida. There you have Gators and Dawgs living together in harmony.

They may not agree on much, but in Lot E of the sports complex next to EverBank Field, these fans turn the Florida-Georgia game into more than just a Saturday event. It used to be that the RV City lot opened on Monday (or midnight Sunday), but the city of Jacksonville pushed that back until noon on the Wednesday before the game.

Fans, though, start to line up in their recreational vehicles on the Sunday before the game. You often see Gator fans and Bulldog fans side-by-side, sharing a common area and cooking together. "Everyone gets along until gameday," said Dave Sapp, a Gators fan from Pensacola, Florida, who has been to RV City several times. "Then the jawing starts. But during the week, the thing I always took away from RV City was the way everyone got along."

It's a long party prior to gameday. The smart fans rent their personal portable toilets and become the most popular fans in their rows. The city sends water trucks to the area every morning to refill the tanks. The city also provides entertainment for the RV City fans. Concerts have become a staple as has a decorating contest. Because the game is usually on Halloween weekend, the outfits tend to fall on the crazy side. Friday is karaoke night, and a party atmosphere occurs every night. "It's really electric," Sapp said. "It's absolutely wild. It's a great time. They make it very convenient and they make a concerted effort to keep everyone there instead of on the road."

Each parking space costs $100 a day, and they are awarded on a first-come, first-serve basis, which is why the RVs start lining up days before the lot opens. For a fan who wants to rent an RV and experience RV City, the cost is about $400 for a Friday-Sunday weekend. For someone truly wanting to experience the happening, it would be more like $800 for Wednesday through Sunday.

Plus, of course, there are the expenditures for food and drink. And there is no shortage of either—until RV City closes at noon on Sunday.

# 99 Best Kicking Combos

Coaches will tell you that special teams are one-third of the game, and that includes coverage and returns. But without a couple of good kickers, special teams can only be so special.

During the 2012 season, Florida had one of the best kicking combinations in the school's history. Caleb Sturgis was money on field goal attempts, making 24-of-28 field goals, and two were blocked because of poor protection. He also had 31 kickoffs that went for touchbacks. Meanwhile, punter Kyle Christy, who won the job midway through the 2011 season, averaged 45.8 yards a punt and had 27 punts downed inside the 20-yard line.

So was that the best combination in Gators history?

Sturgis benefitted from a kickoff rule, starting with the 2012 season, that moved them up five yards, but he also made a school-record eight field goals from 50 yards or longer during his career. Three of those came in 2012.

You could make an argument that Florida was awfully good in the kicking game just three years earlier when Chas Henry averaged 43.4 yards a punt and Sturgis was 22-of-30. Henry had to do it all the following year when Sturgis suffered a back injury. Henry responded by averaging 45.1 yards a kick and kicking the game-winning field goal in overtime against Georgia.

He wasn't the first Gators player to handle both punting and kicking duties—and certainly not the most famous. Steve Spurrier averaged 40.3 yards a punt during 1966, the year he also kicked the 40-yard field goal that beat Auburn and helped him win the Heisman Trophy. But if you are going to rate the best kicking duos in UF history, only two others can compare with the Sturgis-Christy combo of 2012.

Ray Criswell averaged 44.4 yards a punt—the best in school history—during his Florida career from 1982 to 1985. Bobby Raymond was the most accurate kicker in school history at 87.9 percent, though the goal posts were a bit wider than they are now. Raymond also owns the school record with 17 consecutive made field goals. He and Criswell were a big part of Florida's first (and later vacated) SEC title in 1984.

Judd Davis won the Lou Groza Award in 1994 as the nation's best placekicker. Shayne Edge averaged 42.5 yards a punt from 1991 to 1994, including an average of 43.6 in '94. Edge also made a key run for a first down during the 1993 SEC Championship Game. It's difficult to argue with Sturgis as the best Florida kicker ever at because of his range. "Is he the best?" asked Davis, who mentored Sturgis at UF. "He's in the top two." Davis was a walk-on while Edge was recruited out of Columbia High in Lake City, Florida. Or at least…he was recruited as much as Spurrier ever recruited a punter.

On his recruiting visit to Florida, Edge waited patiently outside Spurrier's office while the head ball coach was talking on the phone. Finally director of football operations Jamie Speronis knocked on the door and told Spurrier, "Coach, we have the punter we're trying to recruit out here."

Spurrier replied, "Punter? We don't punt much around here."

Florida, however, has a long history of excellent punters and placekickers. Bobby Joe Greene, John James, and Eric Wilbur were outstanding punters. David Posey, Jeff Chandler, and Berj Yepremian were excellent and accurate kickers.

But the best combo? Considering Florida's conservative offense in 2012, it's hard to beat Sturgis and Christy.

# 100 Visit Tim Tree-bow

It seemed like a good idea at the time. An oak tree, hugging the outdoor patio at the Ballyhoo Grill, had died on University Avenue about a mile from campus. They could yank it out or turn it into a work of art.

Chainsaw artist Sam Knowles liked the latter idea, and Ballyhoo owner Chris Fragale agreed. So Knowles went to work and created a 7½-foot version of Florida quarterback Tim Tebow. At the time Tebow-mania was at an all-time high. The quarterback had won his second national title and wowed a crowd at The Swamp in January of 2009 by announcing, "Let's do it again. I'm coming back."

Therein lay the problem.

The statue did not have a sign that said it was Tebow, but it wore a No. 15 Gators jersey, held a Heisman Trophy in its right hand, and sported eye black. An amusing addition to the Gainesville landscape, it was great for Ballyhoo.

But Florida didn't find it humorous. The University Athletic Association sent a cease-and-desist letter to Ballyhoo because of an NCAA rule that does not allow any likeness of a student-athlete to be used by a business while he or she is still playing, and Tebow still had his senior year left. It didn't matter that the gift shops owned by the UAA could sell No. 15 jerseys by the cartload. The statue had to come down.

Knowles, though, had a better idea. He just changed it from No. 15 to No. 7, Danny Wuerffel's jersey number, in September of 2009. Wuerffel had a Heisman, too, so it worked. That satisfied the powers that be for the interim, and as soon as Tebow's eligibility was up, it was back to No. 15 on the dead oak.

But according to Bill Reichardt, a business partner in the restaurant, you might want to check out Tree-bow quickly if you haven't seen it. He said termites are starting to be an issue.

Ballyhoo is more than just a statue. The restaurant has an SEC theme with menu items such as Kentucky Blue Steak Salad, Razorback Sliders, Bulldawg Bites, and Commodore Crab Soup. You can also try one of their Man vs. Food-like challenges. How about the Mus-Champ where you have to eat a three-pound hamburger stuffed with cheese and bacon and a pound of fries?

Ballyhoo has been a hangout for coaches since it opened in 1998. When Urban Meyer stopped by, he had a special item—mahi mahi bites—served up to him that wasn't on the menu. The radio shows of football coach Will Muschamp, basketball coach Billy Donovan, and volleyball coach Mary Wise each broadcast from there.

And you never know which current or former players will stop by as evidenced by the walls of the restaurant, displaying pictures of some of the greatest Gators ever posing with staff.

# Acknowledgments

When in doubt, ask Uncle Norm. That's the media's nickname for Norm Carlson, the longtime sports information director at Florida who is now the football historian. He has retired more times than a heavyweight boxer. And this book wouldn't have been possible without him.

Steve McClain, the current sports information director at Florida, was a great help as well. And associate athletic directors Mike Hill and Chip Howard can relax, knowing that when my name pops up on their cell phones now it's not a question about the stadium or the F Club. And thanks to my colleague, Robbie Andreu, who has lived through much of this history with me at *The Gainesville Sun*. Robbie and I started going to games as kids, continued in college, and now work together at *The Gainesville Sun*.

I also have to give a shout out to the players and coaches who were more than happy to talk to me. Steve Spurrier, Will Muschamp, and Urban Meyer had no problem taking the time to answer my questions. Players such as Chris Leak, Shane Matthews, Kevin Carter, and Carlos Alvarez were amazing. One thing about covering the Gators, you develop friendships that last forever.

And especially a big thanks to Danny Wuerffel, who wrote the foreword. I think it's really well done. I feel blessed to call Danny my friend.

And finally, thanks to my wife, who pushed me in the right direction on some of the chapters and is thrilled that she no longer has to hear the countdown: "Hey, honey, I just did my 32nd chapter. Only 68 to go."

That had to get old.

# Sources

Almost all of the content of this book came from personal interviews or press conferences attended by the author, as well as his experiences in covering the Gators for 38 years. The Florida football media guide was also a major source of information in compiling this book as were personal interviews with Florida football historian Norm Carlson.

**Other sources:**

Chapter 9: *The Daytona Beach News-Journal*, September 1, 2012.

Chapter 29: *Sports Illustrated*, July 1, 1968.

Chapter 33: *Los Angeles Times*, February 1, 2012.

Chapter 34: University of Florida Foundation and Gatorzone.com.

Chapter 42: *Orlando Sentinel*, November 21, 2008.

Chapter 47: Gatorbowl.com.

Chapter 76: Gatorzone.com and gatortailgating.com.

Chapter 85: *The Gainesville Sun*, August 30, 2010.

Chapter 94: Gatorzone.com.